BLOOD ON THE MITTEN

INFAMOUS MICHIGAN MURDERS

1700s *to* PRESENT

TOM CARR

Dedicated to the victims.

Readers are encouraged to go to www.MissionPointPress.com to find information on how to buy this book in bulk at a discounted rate.

Published by Chandler Lake Books, an Imprint of Mission Point Press

2554 Chandler Lake Rd.
Traverse City, MI 49686

(231) 421-9513

www.MissionPointPress.com

Series editor: Heather Lee Shaw
Book design by Heather Lee Shaw

ISBN: 978-1-943338-07-8

Library of Congress Control Number: 2016939801

Printed in the United States of America.

CHANDLER LAKE
BOOKS

ChandlerLakeBooks.com
Traverse City, MI • Kansas City, MO

CONTENTS

The search for Kathy.
See page 92.

INTRODUCTION

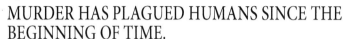

MURDER HAS PLAGUED HUMANS SINCE THE
BEGINNING OF TIME.

It may be something that's in our DNA. Chimpanzees, our
closest relative in the animal kingdom, are believed to kill
each other at about the same rate — based on population — as
humans. Moving forward, it only takes the Old Testament four
chapters before it deals with the important problem of homicide,
and that fratricidal lesson of Cain and Abel appears across
cultures, from the Christian Bible to the Jewish Torah and the
Muslim Quran. Just a few years ago, scientists claimed to have
found evidence of prehistoric murder in a Spanish cave. That
victim was killed about 430,000 years ago with two blows to the
skull, both, apparently, from the same weapon.

But this is not just a book about murder, it's also a book about
Michigan. That has to do with my familiarity with and love for
the state. I was born in Grand Rapids, grew up in Northville,
went to Michigan State University, and have lived and/or worked
in Sturgis, Sault Ste. Marie, Traverse City and Buckley.

That said, Michigan does unfortunately outpace the country in
murder rate. The good news is that the state and national trend
has been downward for decades. Michigan topped out at 13.0
murders per 100,000 people in 1974 and was down to 5.4 per
100,000 in 2014. (In comparison, the U.S. topped out in 1980
with 10.2 per 100,000 and dropped to 4.5 in 2014.) And Detroit
has in the past earned the moniker Murder City for regularly
topping the sad murder statistics, though it's not always sitting at
the summit anymore.

Yet this book isn't about rates. It's about the truly appalling,
the perplexing, the historical killings that have sprung up here
throughout the years. To be sure, some of the people who grace
the pages of this book are among the worst and most vicious
ever to walk on the Wolverine State's sandy soil. Still others are
ordinary people who gave way to passion or insanity. Some killed
for others, others killed for a cause. A few killers in these pages
are unknown, as are some motives.

While I've strived to include the most notorious cases in state history, this book is by no means encyclopedic. I've missed some crimes and locations, for sure. A couple, I admit, would not likely be here if they hadn't occurred near my home. One of them I covered for years as a newspaper reporter.

Also, you may notice a change in tone among some of the older cases as compared with the newer ones. Naturally, it's a bit easier to assume a lighter voice with the older cases as they're distant from our current experience. Despite the grim topic, I've tried to respect the victims above all.

As much as possible, I've also tried to put the reader in the time and place of each case. In so doing, I've taken some liberties — not with facts, but with mood. If I write that someone was shaking or sweating under certain horrifying circumstances, I have no way of knowing that for sure. On the other hand, I've guessed at such details in order to put more, shall we say, flesh and bones on the case than you might find in news accounts. Assumptions in straight news reporting is understandably a no-no.

Further, I've looked closely at the places where the crimes occurred. While I don't believe in good or bad places, I hope evil is through visiting these locations (and all others for that matter).

Hate and horror are not particular to any given time. It often seems that people are worse and the age more dangerous now than ever. Yet a look across time shows that people have always had the capacity to do terrible and evil things. The weapons and the motives change — or not — but the outcome remains the same: people kill people on purpose.

But please don't take that to be a cynical and defeatist view. We've survived through the millennia in spite of the bad eggs. Good people who wouldn't think of taking a human life are, and always have been, in the vast majority.

In fact, that's what makes the truly disgusting and vile occurrences in books like this stand out. Let's hope they are never so commonplace that we become blasé.

TOM CARR

Kathy Radtke's personal effects.
See page 92.

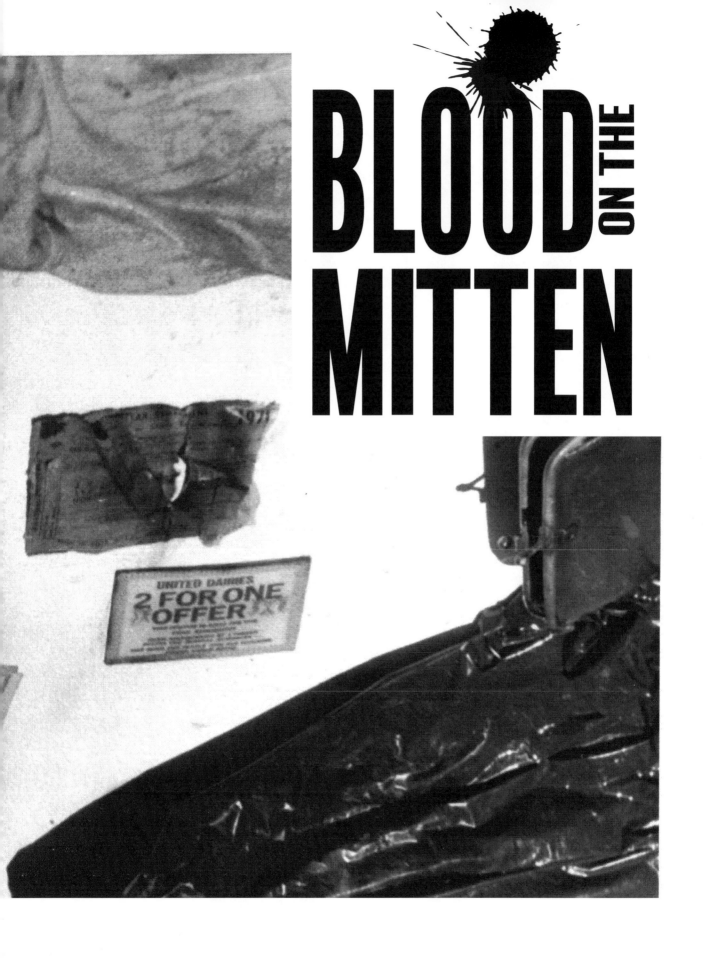

BLOOD ON THE MITTEN

AN EXECUTION TO END EXECUTION

THE YEAR: 1830
THE CRIME: MURDER
THE MOTIVE: NOT KEEPING UP

STEPHEN GIFFORD SIMMONS WAS A TALL, HANDSOME SONOFAGUN.

He seemed to have everything going for him with his firm handshake, his handsome smile, and his deep baritone. But lurking behind it all was the worst kind of bully, and alcohol was just the ingredient to melt his facade.

Too bad Simmons owned a bar, even if it was a dark and broken down place set back in the deep woods off the muddy, rutted Detroit-Chicago Road. In those days, Michigan was a marshy, mosquito-ridden frontier with fewer than 15,000 white settlers. Detroit, which had grown little since its days as a fur-trading settlement and military outpost for New France, was a tiny town of 2,000. Simmons and his family were part of a wave of New York-staters and New Englanders heading out into the wilderness to search for better times and a stake of their own.

One night in 1830, seven years before Michigan became a state, Simmons came into the kitchen with a jug of whiskey and demanded that his wife, Levana, share it with him. He'd take a pull, then hand her the jug. He told her she had to keep up. She tried, but she just couldn't, and said she'd had enough. That really ticked the charming Simmons off, and he punched her so hard she fell to the floor. Dead.

That's the popular account, anyway.

There were hints that the strapping pioneer wife and mother of six wasn't spending all her time washing and scrubbing. There were whispers of hanky-panky. Plus, everyone knew she was as big a drinker as he was, and almost as mean. But on this occasion, he must have caught her off-guard and that first surprise punch led to many more.

The public hanging of Stephen Simmons.

During the trial, his daughters spoke of his horrible temper, and that his family lived in never-ending fear. But what the rest of the town saw was a well-educated, gregarious and likable fellow.

Nevertheless, they sentenced him to hang.

As the day approached, grandstands went up on a triangle of land north of Jefferson Avenue. People rode a day's journey to see the show. They camped out, cooked food, sang and played songs while waiting for the big event. In fact, the hanging of Stephen Gifford Simmons may have been the largest gathering to date in the not-yet-Motor City. The sheriff was so keen on entertaining the death-watchers that he allowed vendors to sell their wares and booked a fife-and-drum band.

Still, the tall, dashing tavern-owner was well-known and well-liked. Some folks had mixed feelings about seeing him die. He also had a beautiful, baritone singing voice which he knew how to use to great effect. As Simmons was escorted to the gallows on September 24, 1830, he began singing hymns with those golden pipes. If he had hoped to forestall his execution, it didn't work. On the other hand, he did succeed in ruining the mood.

Now, you may want to sit down when I tell you that the part about him singing and swinging might not be true either. Well, he did swing. But while the tuneful tale has settled into popular lore, the anti-alcohol crusaders of the late 1800s probably made it up to serve their own political agenda.

True or not, the frontier spectators found the display distasteful enough that in 1846, the legislature abolished the death penalty. Simmons was the last man to hang by order of the state of Michigan, and Michigan was the first government in the English-speaking world to outlaw the death penalty.

MURDER MAP

The carnival-turned-bummer that was Stephen Simmons' hanging took place at **Farmer Street** and **Gratiot Avenue** in downtown Detroit. A branch of the Detroit Public Library sits there now, with a People Mover track overhead. There's not much present that harkens back to the macabre scene of Simmons' hanging, though it is kind of cool that the layout of the streets has remained the same.

Simmons' tavern was right in the middle of downtown Wayne, a Ford company town a few miles north of Detroit Metro Airport. And the Detroit-Chicago trail/road, originally the Sauk Trail, is part of the Michigan Avenue that runs west through the state and into Chicago. There's a historical marker at **35118 Michigan Avenue**, in the city of Wayne, on the facade of a golden brick building with a clock on top.

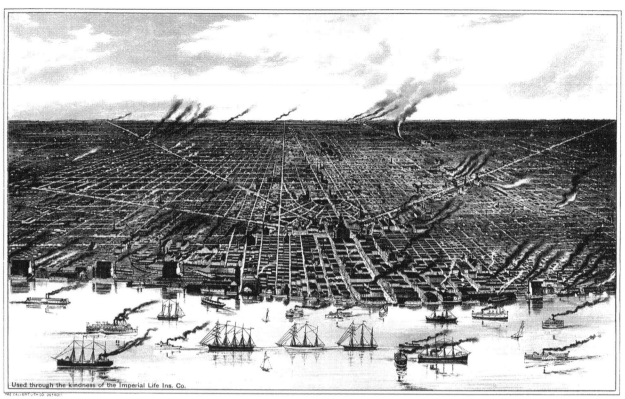

Used through the kindness of the Imperial Life Ins. Co.

BIRDS EYE VIEW — SHOWING ABOUT THREE MILES SQUARE — OF THE CENTRAL PORTION OF THE CITY OF DETROIT, MICHIGAN.

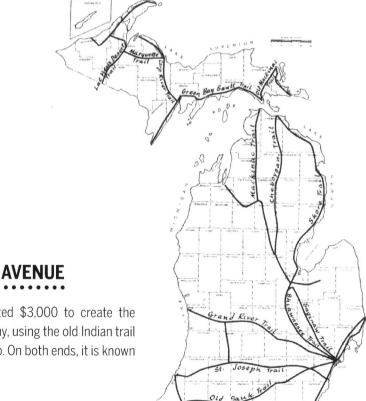

MICHIGAN AVENUE
• • • • • • • • • • • • • • • • • • •

In 1825, Congress appropriated $3,000 to create the nation's second federal highway, using the old Indian trail that linked Detroit and Chicago. On both ends, it is known as Michigan Avenue.

HEAD TO TOE

THE YEAR: 1929
THE CRIME: MURDER
THE MOTIVE: ONLY A CLAIRVOYANT WOULD KNOW

BENNY EVANGELIST HAD JUST FINISHED HIS OPUS, THE OLDEST HISTORY OF THE WORLD DISCOVERED BY OCCULT SCIENCE IN DETROIT, MICHIGAN, WHEN SOMEONE CHOPPED HIS HEAD OFF WITH AN AXE AND SET IT AT HIS FEET.

In fact, Benny may have divined that his days were numbered, as he was ready to skip town for a farm in Marine City, northeast of Detroit on the St. Clair River. The real estate agent who closed the deal found his headless client and the rest of his dead family when he came to collect the first mortgage payment.

Benny, an Italian immigrant from Naples, came to the United States in his teens as Benjamino Evangelista. He dropped the last 'a' of his surname to more clearly describe his calling to English speakers. His particular brand of spirituality was a salad of Christianity, Judaism, Voodoo and Satanism, with a lot of herbs and spirit readings tossed in. While the cops never found his killer, there were plenty of suspects as his standard fee for a reading was $10 — about 140 bucks in today's market.

Police found the Evangelist house cluttered with boxes of papers, trinkets and items of clothing. Women's underwear — each tagged with the owner's name — seemed to be of particular importance in Benny's connection to the unseen. A trail of bloody footprints led the police to a suspect, but he was later released for lack of evidence.

Detroit's promise of factory-work riches had increased its population from 285,000 in 1910 to 1.5 million in 1929, most of the newcomers arriving from the South or from overseas. Benny's fate may have been part of a trend of foreign "cult murders," as the papers reported at the time. It may have been revenge for gouging. Or those boxes of women's underwear may have played into it. Whatever the reason, his family paid the ultimate price.

SIX VICTIMS OF DETROIT AX MURDERER

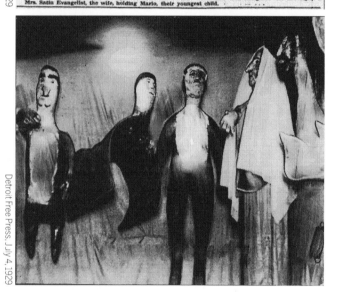

Here are Paul Evangelist, said to have been the head of an Italian religious cult at Detroit, and his wife and four children who were brutally slain by an ax man as they slept. Evangelist is shown at the left with his oldest daughter, Angeline; while below them are Jeanne and Margaret. At the right is Mrs. Satin Evangelist, the wife, holding Mario, their youngest child.

Detroit Free Press, July 4, 1929

Detroit Free Press, July 4, 1929

Benny's paper mache "gods" found at the Evangelist residence by police.

MURDER MAP

The Evangelista home was at **3587 St. Aubin**, among neighborhoods with huge gaps where homes used to be. It's a few blocks north of Eastern Market, a busy, walkable collection of cafes, specialty food stores and farm markets, with local art and music adding flavor, in historic commercial buildings.

CULT MURDERS IN THE 20s & 30s

Benny Evangelist wasn't the only one dabbling with demons in the D during the Prohibition and Depression eras. Take black cult leader Robert Harris, for example. He led a group he called Order of Islam, to the consternation of another much larger group of the same name.

Harris claimed he was ordered by gods to remove "unbeliever" James Smith from the premises. With Smith's hands held high, he marched him up the staircase of their shared home. Then, with Smith's wife watching under threat of death, Harris stabbed the apostate with a silver knife. Not convinced of a successful sacrifice, he followed that up with some Motor City-flavored bashing with a car axle.

MURDER MAP

Harris' Order of Islam had about 100 followers, but another Order of Islam at **3408 Hastings Street** claimed thousands. The site, a few blocks east of the New Center (**Woodward** at **West Grand Boulevard**), is now a vacant field next to a packaging company, overlooking the cloverleaf where the **Edsel Ford Freeway** meets the **Chrysler Freeway**. This area was once a lively African American district, but the vibrant neighborhood was wiped out in the 1960s in the name of transportation progress. The neighborhood was known as Black Bottom because of the rich soil there.

The home at **1429 Dubois** where Harris killed Smith is gone, and would have been somewhere around where University Prep Science & Math Elementary School is now.

THE MISTRESS AND THE GHOST

THE YEAR: 1928
THE CRIME: MURDER
THE MOTIVE: "G" DRIVES HIM CRAZY

WHEN DR. FRANK LOOMIS, DRENCHED IN BLOOD, RAN INTO THE POLICE STATION ON FEB. 27, 1927, AND REPORTED THAT HE'D FOUND HIS WIFE, GLADYS, BLUDGEONED TO DEATH ON THE FLOOR OF THEIR HOME, IT WAS HARD NOT TO RAISE AN EYEBROW.

He'd just stepped out for 45 minutes, he told the police, and when he returned, she was dead, murdered. The blood got on him when he embraced her in his shock and grief.

But why would anyone kill the doctor's wife? Did they steal anything? No.

Making matters more suspicious, when the police rushed to the doctor's Marlowe Avenue home, they found the murder weapon, a 2x4 wooden stake, smoldering in the furnace.

Frank Loomis was charged with murder, and the case became a nationwide tabloid sensation.

During the highly publicized trial, it was revealed that Dr. Loomis had a mistress named Gertrude Newell. The prosecution tried hard to convince the jury that Gertrude was the motive for murder, but there just wasn't enough evidence, and the jury acquitted him.

So much for that. But the doctor's troubles were only beginning. After the acquittal, he moved in with Gertrude, but none of it was coming up roses. Loomis reportedly became despondent — worried about money, and about the fact that he couldn't sell the home where his wife was killed. He also discovered that a mistress is not a wife — Gertrude was no drudge. She wanted a life of "blind pigs, cabarets" and other evening entertainments that the doctor just wasn't up for.

Queer Love Tangle Unsolved By Suicide Of Harassed Man Acquitted Of Slaying Wife

By BONITA WITT

DETROIT, Mich., June 1.—Detroit police are pondering over one of the queerest cases in their history—the Loomis-Newell triangle.

Dr. Frank R. Loomis, physician, is dead—a suicide.

His wife was found murdered in the sunroom of the Loomis home in February, 1927.

Only Mrs. Gertrude Newell pretty divorcee and sweetheart of the doctor, survives.

The Tragedy Begins

It has been more than a year since Dr. Loomis ran to a police station near his home, stammering an almost incoherent story of finding his wife horribly beaten and lifeless less than an hour after he had left her to go for a walk.

While the two Loomis children slept in a nearby room undisturbed, their mother, a powerful woman was cruelly murdered. Apparently a tiny canary was the only witness to the crime, except its perpetrator.

A few days later Dr. Loomis was taken into custody and accused of the crime. A jury acquitted the doctor, but public opinion refused to exonerate him. Until the day of his recent suicide he was a marked man. In the theatre, on the street, in restaurants, people pointed him out to their friends and whispered as he passed.

Only a few remained loyal to him.

At the time of the trial Mrs. Newell was held for a period by police, who said they believed her the "motive" for the murder. They were not able to establish this—both the doctor and Mrs. Newell insisting that their relations had been only that of physician and patient.

Three Stand By

Frequently after the acquittal, Mrs. Newell, Dr. Loomis, Dr. Kesztany and Kolar would sit around the table in a little Hungarian restaurant, listening to gypsy music and talking. The doctor would...

DR. FRANK LOOMIS TOLD POLICE HE FOUND WIFE MURDERED.   ARRESTED AN ACQUITTED OF THE CRIME.   SEEN MUCH IN THE COMPANY OF MRS. GERTRUDE NEWELL.   FEARED MRS. NEWELL WOULD RETURN TO PARENTS. IS SUICIDE.   PROSTRATED, MRS. NEWELL EVADES POLICE AND REPORTERS.

So, less than a year later, in the same home where his wife had been so savagely killed, the doctor closed the doors and windows, stuck the end of a two-foot gas burner into his mouth and asphyxiated himself. He left two suicide notes. One stated that he was innocent of his wife's murder. The other said, enigmatically, "G. drives me crazy."

It was never really clear which of his two women he was referring to.

MURDER MAP

Marlowe Avenue, where the Loomises lived and Gladys was found beaten to death, runs north to south on the city's west side. The Loomis address was **13901 Marlowe Street**, on the corner with **Schoolcraft Avenue**, near **Grand River Avenue**. There's a home still standing that would appear to be the one where the murder and suicide both occurred.

Dr. Loomis's practice was in the Freeman Building, closer to downtown and the old Tiger Stadium at **3626 Grand River Avenue**, an address that no longer exists, between a branch of the Detroit Public Library and I Am My Brother's Keeper Ministries.

BURNING DOWN THE HOUSE

THE YEAR: 1977
THE CRIME: MURDER
THE MOTIVE: ABUSE

FRANCINE HUGHES WAS SICK OF BEING BEATEN, BRUISED, AND HUMILIATED BY HER EX-HUSBAND JAMES "MICKEY" HUGHES.

She was tired of explaining away black eyes to neighbors and the children. She'd had 13 years of accepting the heavy fist of his frustrations.

She fell in love with him at age 16 and begged her parents to let her marry the brooding boy, two years her senior. A few weeks later, when she came home with new clothes, he tore them off her in a rage. Were they too pretty? Too provocative? Who knows, but she apologized. And so it went. Pregnancy followed quickly, and the kids became the reason for staying married. There was a history there — Francine's mother was married to the same kind of abuser and stayed married for the same reason.

When the fourth child arrived, and Francine found herself without food or rent money, she filed for divorce. But Mickey refused to move out. He'd barge in whenever he wanted to smack her around before flopping down for a drunken snooze.

After a car accident left Mickey in a coma, Francine allowed him back home to recover. Recover he did, although he refused to look for work, criticizing her brutally for everything from meals to her attempts to educate herself. The beatings became more regular, and lasted longer. Francine thought of killing herself to escape him…but then who would take care of the kids?

March 9 may have been a day like any other, but it was the last day. There was yelling and hair-pulling, punching and smashed dishes. Mickey made her burn her school books and threatened to take a sledgehammer to her car. After insisting on sex, he fell asleep. Francine heard a little voice say, "Do it."

She bundled up the kids and herded them out to the car. Then she came back inside and poured gasoline around the bed where Mickey slept, tossed a match on it, then ran out to the kids in the car. She has been quoted as saying: "I was as calm as though I were doing an ordinary thing. I felt very light, clear-headed, free. This was the easiest thing I had ever done."

As flames spread through the home, she drove to Mason, to the sheriff's office, and confessed, "I did it."

Her case seemed to speak to the many women trapped in abusive marriages — not to commit murder, but as a cry for help for women in dangerous relationships. Protesters gathered outside her trial in Lansing, and her case inspired new efforts to protect women from domestic violence. Francine was acquitted of the crime and became a symbol for better prosecution of spouse beaters.

MURDER MAP

Dansville is a village surrounded by farms, about 25 miles southeast of Lansing. Mason is the Ingham county seat, though Lansing and East Lansing are the largest cities in the county.

Real Life in Film
• • • • • • • • • • • • • • •

The issue of spousal abuse was truly pushed into the spotlight, and onto the daytime talk shows, when NBC TV released a movie in 1984 titled "The Burning Bed." The movie starred 1970s pinup Farrah Fawcett as Francine.

HEAD ON A PLATTER

THE YEAR: 1897
THE CRIME: MURDER
THE MOTIVE: THE VOICES IN HER HEAD

THE WORD GOT AROUND IN WILLIAMSTON: ON THE OTHER SIDE OF THE RAILROAD TRACK IS THE MOST HIDEOUS THING YOU'LL EVER SEE.

Alfy Haney was there first. It was his house, after all, and he was dragging his disappointment home with him after another unsuccessful day of hunting for work. Surprisingly, the door was wide open. And there, on the dining room table, on a plate, with a knife and fork to either side, was his mother's head.

Was it a message, or was the killer insane?

Whichever it was, the townspeople crowded around the doorway as the sheriff settled his queasiness and picked the head up off the platter. The head and the room it had sat in were in bad shape. Both had taken a beating. Both were covered with trails and splatters of blood.

Then they found the rest of the body. It was around the corner, charred almost beyond recognition.

The slight, mousy daughter-in-law, Martha Haney, copped to the murder on the spot and was arrested.

People around town had known for awhile that there was something nasty cooking at the Haney residence. Men who worked at the barrel stave factory next door often heard Martha arguing bitterly with her mother-in-law. And folks knew that Martha talked to the dead — her dead mother, that is. Her husband had even been to a doctor to get advice on what to do about it.

Something snapped on an April morning in 1897. Martha went behind the house, found the razor-sharp axe, and returned to the house. Maybe her mother-in-law suspected the attack, since she had locked the door. No problem. Martha chopped it down. Then she chopped down Mariah Haney.

The only real question to be determined in the grisly case was whether Martha was sane. After lengthy examinations — the killer wavering between saying her mother told her to do it and not remembering what she'd done — authorities determined that she was indeed mentally ill. They blamed poverty and genetics.

Martha was put on a train to the Michigan Asylum for the Dangerous and Criminal Insane in Ionia. Less than a year and a half later, she died of tuberculosis. Today, it's believed she would be diagnosed as schizophrenic.

MURDER MAP

Williamston is a picturesque town east of Lansing, with many of the century-plus-old homes and buildings still standing. The Haneys' home, at **320 Elevator Street**, stood until the 1990s, when firefighters burned it down as part of a training exercise.

Abandoned now, the Ionia hospital treated the mentally ill and the criminally insane until 1972.

NEGATIVE ENERGY

THE YEAR: 2011
THE CRIME: MURDER
THE MOTIVE: AVOIDING ARMAGEDDON

TO MOST PEOPLE WHO KNEW SHIRLEY "MELINDA" MEEKS, SHE WAS A QUIET, 60-ISH, MOTHERLY PRESENCE WHO LIKED TO SEW.

She lived in Reed Manor, a Jackson city-owned and subsidized housing complex with other seniors, people with disabilities and residents with low income.

Leo Kwaske's disability was psychological. He suffered from schizophrenia and paranoia. He was also Melinda's upstairs neighbor. And he didn't see a kindly, unassuming and ordinary woman when he looked at her. He saw and felt "negative energy."

One October morning, a neighbor passed by Meeks' apartment and noticed her door open. Blood was splattered everywhere, even out into the hallway. She nervously looked inside, discovering Melinda's headless body on the floor.

Later that day, Kwaske, who had engineering degrees from Michigan Tech and Purdue, was found walking around in drag. The police got a search warrant and found a bloody hammer in his backpack. Upon further investigation, they also found Melinda's head, washed clean, in his apartment.

Kwaske admitted to using the hammer to break through Meeks' apartment door to take care of her "dark voodoo" for good. He claimed to have spoken with Meeks after her death, through mental powers that allowed him to communicate with good and evil forces. Other voices had ordered him to kill Meeks, he said, and to cut off her head so she couldn't regenerate. "I needed to stop her or she would cause Armageddon," he told doctors. "It was not vengeance. I was just stopping something that was dangerous to the world and to me."

Kwaske was found not guilty by reason of insanity, but he is expected to spend the rest of his life in mental institutions.

MURDER MAP

Reed Manor is at **301 Steward Avenue** in Jackson, just northwest of the center of town.

BLOWING THE CASE SKY HIGH

THE YEAR: 1936
THE CRIME: MURDER
THE MOTIVE: DON'T TAKE MY GUN

RAYMOND KIVELA WAS A 27-YEAR-OLD TRAPPER WHO LIVED WITH HIS PARENTS IN THE CENTRAL UPPER PENINSULA.

Slight, bespectacled and bad tempered, he'd learned to keep an eye out for conservation officers while wandering the rough terrain just north of Negaunee and Ishpeming. But that's not why he had his .22-caliber rifle with him when he was checking traps that crisp October day. He had his gun just in case he saw a squirrel, or something else that might make a nice dinner.

While hiking the rocky, rooty trail, he happened to run into Officer Andrew Schmeltz. Schmeltz, one of the more inflexible officers of the area, had driven out from Negaunee, following complaints about illegal muskrat traps. The officer never got around to asking Raymond about the traps. First, he wanted to see the young man's license for the .22.

"It's at home," Raymond said, pointing his thumb toward town.

Schmeltz held out his hand, asking for the gun so he could look it over. Raymond started to hand it to him, then changed his mind and shoved the officer on his rear end. As Schmeltz started to get up, Raymond panicked and fired two shots into his chest at close range. It was only a .22, but he must have been unlucky enough to land the bullet in a lethal spot. He'd acted without thinking and then realized, to his horror, that Schmeltz was dead.

Raymond dropped the gun and dragged Schmeltz's body into a swamp. He covered it over with leaves, brush, whatever he could find. But he knew that wasn't enough. Someone would miss the guy, and soon. What he needed was some…dynamite. He picked some up at the hardware store on the way home.

That evening, he fidgeted through dinner, then lay awake until his parents slept and he could safely sneak out and take care of business. Seventy sticks of dynamite — that's right, seven-zero — were placed around the body of Officer Schmeltz, surely enough to obliterate the evidence.

And it looked like it might work: the huge blast lit up the night, sending rocks, water and everything else flying for the radius of a football field. But after the dust and debris settled…horrors. It hadn't worked at all the way he thought it would. Now, bits of human flesh and scalp, underwear and uniform fragments, legs and intestine hung from the swampy trees and scrub bushes all over the place.

The solution? More dynamite!

Two more charges were set, which may have thinned out the bloody mess, but it didn't erase it.

Kivela eventually confessed and was sentenced to life in prison. He grew old in Michigan penitentiaries, Newberry State Hospital and finally, a nursing home.

The prosecutor in the case was John Voelker, who would go on to write *Anatomy of a Murder* about another case from his legal career.

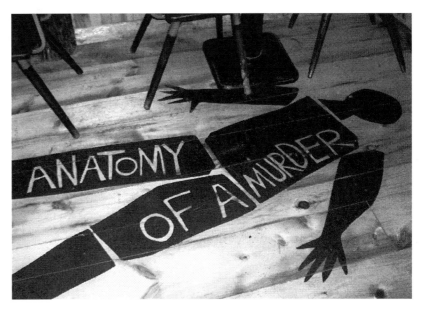

Anatomy of a Murder
• •

John D. Voelker was named to the Michigan Supreme Court right about the time his book, published under the pen name Robert Traver, became a bestseller and was turned into a movie.

The book, Anatomy of a Murder, was based on a murder case from his legal career, in which an army lieutenant was accused of killing a bar owner who had allegedly raped his wife.

The movie was shot in Marquette and premiered in 1959. Its cast included James Stewart and George C. Scott. Duke Ellington composed the musical score. It's considered by some to be one of the finest depictions of courtroom drama in cinema history.

MURDER MAP

Negaunee and Ishpeming are west of Marquette. The Carp River runs for just over 20 miles, and is a largely unspoiled stream prized by outdoor sports enthusiasts. It also has some waterfalls that are said to be difficult to reach but worth the effort.

A Big Gray Wolf in the Snow
Caught and Held in two No. 2, Steel Traps
Feet Frozen but no less Painful

Yes, He killed Cattle, to Eat, But,
Did He Deserve This?
A Big Wolf in a No. 4 steel trap

A journal entry by American naturalist Vernon Orlando Bailey, 1909-1918.

Beaver hat styles
from the late 1700s
to mid-1800s.

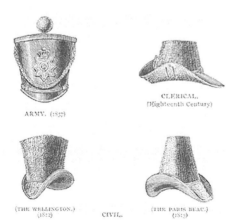

ARMY. (1837)

CLERICAL.
(Eighteenth Century)

(THE WELLINGTON.)
(1812)

CIVIL.

(THE PARIS BEAU.)
(1815)

A Kingdom for a Hat

When Antoine Laumet de La Mothe, sieur de Cadillac landed his canoes in 1701, he put Detroit on the map. Literally. "Le detroit" in French means The Strait.

Cadillac wasn't the first Frenchman to nose his canoes into Michigan rivers. That had been going on since 1535, and there were already half a dozen forts set up on Michigan's Great Lakes: Sault Ste. Marie (1668), Fort de Baude at Saint Ignace (1686), Fort Saint Joseph (Port Huron (1686), Saint Joseph (1679), and Niles (1691).

The forts were there to keep out the British, but they were also trading posts, and the primary — and most coveted product — was fur.

They say that Cadillac founded Detroit so King Louis XIV could wear a fur hat. It's not that far off the truth. Cadillac staked out a village on The Strait, between the Detroit and Savoyard rivers (the Savoyard was lost to Detroit's sewer system in the 1800s), chopped down the trees and built a fort. Then he invited the Indians to trade. They came, and soon the pelts of beaver, bear, wolf, elk, deer, opossum, marten, raccoon, fox, lynx, muskrat and mink were shipping out for King Louis.

For more than a hundred years, the fur trade flourished in Michigan. You'll never guess what killed it: silk. In 1824, silk hats became the fashion statement and fur took a dive. At that point, Louis XIV was long dead, and his great-grandson had lost his head to the guillotine.

BOOK BOMB

THE YEAR: 1967
THE CRIME: MURDER
THE MOTIVE: RESTAURANT ENVY

THE TASTY CAFE IN MARSHALL HAD NO PRETENSIONS TO FINE CUISINE.

One of those inside-lighted plastic signs with the Tasty name below the Vernors logo was a simple way of letting diners know whose brand of pop would tickle their nose while they waited on their cheeseburger and fries.

On the muggy summer morning of August 18, 1967, a few minutes after nine, the mailman came in during his daily rounds and handed a brown paper package marked "BOOKS" to proprietor Nola Puyear. As a couple of customers ate their breakfasts, she went behind the counter and tore into the package, paused for a second and muttered, "oh!"

A bomb blasted out from the parcel and sent bloody chunks of Nola in every direction, destroying the rear of the restaurant, blowing out the front windows and raining glass out onto the town's main street, Michigan Avenue. (Yep. That road again.)

What was going on? An unremarkable diner in a small town had been inexplicably destroyed. But more shockingly, the kindly owner, known and loved by much of the town, was very, very dead.

Another bombshell, so to speak, would soon rock the town.

Paul Puyear, Nola's husband, was the first real suspect, and his alleged motive was sex. Detectives discovered a clandestine trailer parked two hours north in Barryton, where the husband of motherly Nola carried on sexual affairs with women and men. The titillating secrets rocked Marshall's image of the folksy couple, married 38 years, who still had their Arkansas accents. If they were hiding secrets, then who else?

But the investigation hit a roadblock. If Paul had sent the bomb, it would have been death to him as well. He was in the diner when the book bomb arrived, standing just a few feet from his wife.

Another shocker surfaced. The police discovered that Nola received pills for her nerves through the mail, and one recent delivery included a dose poisoned with Drano. Her nerves must have been strong those days as she didn't swallow any, but the discovery at least got the police off the husband's back.

The big break came when someone contacted a *Detroit News* secret witness line to say they recognized the handwriting on a fragment of the bomb parcel's packaging, which had been reproduced in the paper. That secret someone had the right guy. It was Enoch Chism, a violent wife-beater and arsonist with whom the police were already familiar.

Turns out, Chism had wanted to buy the Tasty Cafe, but the Puyears weren't selling. Well, the sexy husband was all for it, but Nola held out. It was the strongest motive the police and prosecutor had to go on, and it won them a conviction. Chism went to jail.

But that's not the end of the story. Enoch Chism appealed, and the court spent precious time debating whether he was wealthy enough to hire his own lawyer. They dithered themselves right into a release for violation of the Sixth Amendment to the U.S. Constitution: "[i]n all criminal prosecutions, the accused shall enjoy the right to a speedy…trial…"

In this case, though, once a criminal, always a criminal. Chism died in 1979, awaiting another trial for a planned armed robbery.

Nerve Pills

The Sixties are remembered for free love and rock-n-roll, but don't forget the drugs. The kids who went to Woodstock were all raised on vitamins, vaccines, antibiotics and fortified foods like Tang and Wonderbread. The Flower Children were used to pills and needles, but they chose an herb — a crude drug (see page 71) — as their psychotrope of choice. Their parents were the real pill-poppers.

In fact, the decade was the dawn of what could be called The Pharmaceutical Age. The polio vaccine breakthrough of the 50s was put in sugar cubes for school children, the birth-control pill hit the market and Valium and Librium became "mother's little helper," like in the Rolling Stones song of that name. Doctors wrote prescriptions with abandon. According to the Canadian Government Commission of Inquiry into the Nonmedical Use of Drugs (1972), "In 1965 in the USA, some 58 million new prescriptions and 108 million refills were written for psychotropes (sedatives, tranquilizers, and stimulants), and these 166 million prescriptions accounted for 14% of the total prescriptions of all kinds written in the United States."

MURDER MAP

The Tasty Cafe was at **209 East Michigan Avenue**. Marshall is known as the home of popular restaurant Win Schuler's.

Full of grand old homes from the 1800s, Marshall boasts one of the largest historic landmark districts in the nation.

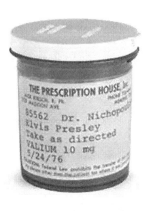

WHISKEY (AND BLOOD) RIVER

THE YEAR: 1918 – 1933
THE CRIME: MURDER
THE MOTIVE: MONEY AND POWER

IT'S BEEN SAID THAT PROHIBITION WAS THE BIGGEST GIFT THE GOVERNMENT EVER GAVE TO ORGANIZED CRIME.

And Detroit's criminals got a 20-month jump on the rest of the country's mobsters, as booze became illegal here on May 1, 1918.

Michigan was well positioned geographically to become Bootleg Central. Although Canada had its own laws against the consumption of alcohol, wineries, breweries and distilleries were allowed to stay open for the export market. No need to fire up a still when there were factory-sized distilleries churning out crates of fire-water a half-mile over the Detroit River. Old Log Cabin whiskey was the primary Canadian import.

The Detroit–Windsor border became a sort of Laredo–Juarez of Prohibition days. When night fell, anyone who owned a boat and was willing to quietly cross over from Belle Isle (or the narrow passages upriver) could fill up and score a lot of cash. During the winter months, there was even a regular parade of cars risking the perilous drive over thin ice. On occasion, one bootlegger would move a rival's track markers, steering them toward a thin patch. There are said to be a number of early model Detroit wheels and bootlegger skeletons at rest in the river muck.

But thin ice caused barely a hiccup in the flow of booze heading into Michigan. Police records from the era suggest that as much as 75% of all illegal liquor imported into the United States arrived through Detroit. So in January of 1920, when Prohibition started for the rest of the country, where did Al Capone look to slake the thirsts of the Windy City? Detroit, of course. Motor City outlaws already had its supply and distribution chains well-established.

There's no central figure like Chicago's Capone in Detroit's early mobster lore, but there is the Purple Gang, the city's dominant crime syndicate of the 1920s and 30s. The Purples came from the Hastings Street section of Detroit's lower east side and were led by Sam Kert and Sammie "Purple" Coen, plus four notorious brothers — Abe, Joe, Ray and Isadore "Izzy" Bernstein, sons of Harry Bernstein, a shoemaker from Russia. Supposedly they'd all been together at the Bishop Union School, a vocational school for delinquents.

By the time Capone looked to expand out of Chicago, the teen-aged Purples had already made a name for themselves with the local cops. They did it by helping themselves to unguarded cargo in local freight yards, threatening people for protection money plus other small-time scams and general violence. Prohibition added fuel to the fire. Capone reportedly feared a war — and bad business — so he struck a deal rather than set up his own Detroit franchise.

Nobody knows for sure how the gang got its Purple name. Some figure it had to do with their ties to the cleaning and dyeing industry, while others point to a judge who once said they were just plain bad, like purple, spoiled meat.

MURDER MAP

The address at **401 Gratiot Avenue**, a mere three blocks from where Stephen Simmons was hanged (page 10), is where the Bernsteins' patriarch raised his family on the salary of a cobbler.

Take a short walk to the north and you'll run into Comerica Park and Ford Field, as well as Music Hall and the Detroit Opera House. A couple blocks south is Greektown.

The Fort Shelby Hotel (above) on **525 West Lafayette Boulevard** is where Capone contracted with the Purples in 1927 to import Canadian Club whiskey. They also decided to give the import a homespun name, and it became Old Log Cabin. The hotel, restored in 2008, is now a Hilton.

At the time the Purples were honing their criminal chops, their father toiled at his shop on the edge of the large Jewish ghetto that stretched from **Jefferson Avenue** to **East Grand Boulevard**, over three miles.

The Bishop Union School is now gone. It was at **Winder** and **Hastings**, two streets that no longer meet, as the cloverleaf where **I-75** and **I-375** come together has long since occupied that site.

The Ford International Weekly

THE DEARBORN INDEPENDENT

Dearborn, Michigan, September 3, 1921

The Peace Dove's Chances in Washington

The Peril of Baseball— "Too Much Jew"

"Only Gentiles Need Apply"

As Detroit made its name through modern, industrial achievements, it also gained a less than savory reputation through social and cultural blight. Racism and antisemitism may have been common features of the American cultural landscape in the 20th century, but their malevolence in Detroit was particularly nasty.

There was Henry Ford's anti-Jewish newspaper, the Dearborn Independent, during the 1920s. Ford even had car dealerships around the country push the paper, but closed it in 1927 due to lawsuits.

In the 30s, the Ku Klux Klan splinter group, the Black Legion, had a membership of more than 20,000. Opposing Catholics, Negroes and Jews, the secret vigilante group spread intimidation and violence on their night rides. Like the Klan, they covered their identities. The Legion's robes were black, instead of white like the KKK.

Father Charles Coughlin was a national cheerleader for antisemitism during the 30s, with his vitriolic radio broadcasts from Detroit to as many as 30 million listeners nationwide. Another clergyman, Gerald L.K. Smith, spread the hate on the Protestant side.

Detroit's German American Bund was founded in 1924, and in the 30s American flags flew alongside Adolf Hitler banners. Employment ads from department store J.L. Hudson's read "Only Gentiles need apply." Of course, most public swimming pools did not allow Jews to swim, and there were restrictive covenants preventing them from purchasing or renting houses in Pleasant Ridge, Grosse Pointe and Birmingham.

Purple Gang founders, Sam Kert (left) and Sammie "Purple" Cohen. Cohen's fate is unknown, but Kert retired to Palm Springs and lived into his 90s.

INTRODUCING THE TOMMY GUN

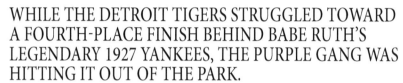

THE YEAR: 1928
THE CRIME: MURDER
THE MOTIVE: SETTLING THE SCORE

WHILE THE DETROIT TIGERS STRUGGLED TOWARD A FOURTH-PLACE FINISH BEHIND BABE RUTH'S LEGENDARY 1927 YANKEES, THE PURPLE GANG WAS HITTING IT OUT OF THE PARK.

As it was for Ruth, 1927 was a year that helped cement the Purple legend. They now were so powerful that they could brazenly assassinate their targets right out in the open. Plus, they'd stood up to Capone. The Detroit River was theirs, they said, but they'd be happy to keep the spigot flowing for him, as long as it was on their terms.

That year, nine upper-level Purple gangsters, including two Bernsteins, were arrested. None of their charges stuck, as usual, and they emerged all the stronger because of it.

By early 1928, though, the Jewish Purples were getting some bootlegging competition from the Italians and Irish. A kind of mob war had broken out, with double-crosses and revenge killings (see page 39). When the Purples ordered a hit to get even for the death of saloon keeper and liquor agent Johnny Reid, they also introduced a deadly new technology to organized crime in Detroit: the machine gun.

Frank Wright was a mobster who'd come to town from Chicago with the now-offensive nickname "Frankie the Pollack". He was also something of a kidnapping expert. While many believed he arrived with the express purpose of killing Johnny Reid, that was two years ago and he was still hanging around. When Frankie popped a long-time Purple drug peddler on the North End, well, that was that.

Frankie was summoned to Apartment 308 of the Miraflores building at 4:45 in the morning on March 27, 1928, supposedly to negotiate the release of a hostage. As he and two other gang members knocked on the door of the apartment, three gunmen burst through the fire door and blasted away. The sound of machine gun fire echoed through the hallway as neighboring tenants hid behind furniture for what must have seemed like forever.

When the shooting stopped, two of the men were dead, turned to hamburger. Wright actually lived through the barrage, until the next day. But it was long enough to tell the cops what had happened. His words were, "The machine gun worked. That's all I can remember." Of course, the gunners got away, and no one was ever charged.

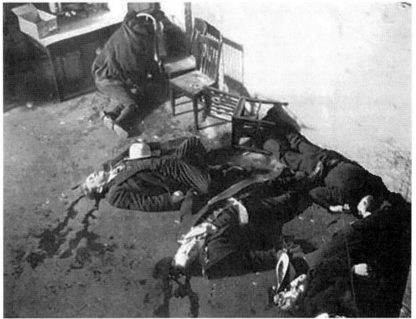

Crime in Detroit, 1920s.

The Tommy Gun

The Tommy gun was invented by John T. Thompson in 1918, just in time for Prohibition. While the Miraflores Massacre was its Detroit debut, it was already well-known in Chicago.

United States Postal workers received the gun first, to fight off increasing mail robberies, and it became available to civilians in 1921. But the gun was expensive — half the cost of a brand new Ford. The Marines got a lot of kick out of it though, using it in the Banana Wars in Central America and in the Caribbean. The Irish Republican Army also flashed the Tommy, as did the Mexican rebel armies. Neither were impressed: you had to get too close to the target to get any effect. Nonetheless, it was just the ticket for spraying a rapid rain of lead into an apartment hallway.

General John T. Thompson holding his invention.

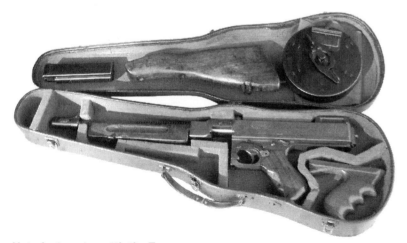

Not playing nice with the Tommy gun.

MURDER MAP

The Miraflores Apartments were at **106 East Alexandrine**. There are now senior apartments in that area. Detroit Receiving Hospital is still just down the block. That's where Wright lingered and died after the attack. The hospital was established in 1915 by the city to serve anyone, regardless of their ability to pay. Needless to say, the modern structure there now does not look like the hospital in which Wright died.

MAKING WAVES ON THE AIRWAVES

THE YEAR: 1930
THE CRIME: MURDER
THE MOTIVE: TALKING TRASH

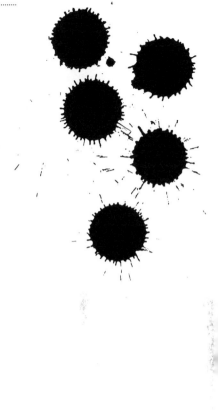

RADIO PERSONALITY JERRY BUCKLEY, BROADCASTING FOR WMBC IN DETROIT, WAS THE CITY'S MOST FAMOUS AND POPULAR CRITIC OF THE LOCAL MOB, AND OF MAYOR CHARLES BOWLES.

Buckley was a native of the Irish neighborhood Corktown, said to be the oldest in the city. He graduated law school and, in 1930, was just beginning a career in radio. One of his favorite topics was accusing Mayor Bowles of cozying up to organized crime. He had plenty of fodder, since gang activity was particularly intense and public that summer. He also blasted Bowles for firing Police Commissioner Harold Emmons, saying it was because Emmons had actually been doing his job: ordering raids on mob businesses and hangouts.

Buckley's daily diatribes from a studio in the mezzanine of the LaSalle Hotel must have had an effect. Bowles served only six months as mayor before citizens demanded a recall election.

And Buckley began receiving regular death threats for his radio commentary. He was undeterred and kept hammering at the sins of the mayor and the mob.

On July 22, Mayor Bowles lost the recall election. That very day, Buckley's wife received a phone call telling her that she would never see her husband again. Sure enough, as he sat in the LaSalle lobby after midnight, reading a newspaper, three hit men quietly walked up to Buckley and killed him, execution style. Twelve bullets were shot, only one missed its mark.

As a popular voice of the people — or what he called the "common herd" on his broadcasts — over 100,000 admirers filed through the Buckley home on Pasadena Avenue to pay their respects. Father Charles Coughlin (see page 29) was an admirer and spoke at his funeral: "The voice of Jerry Buckley was lifted on behalf of those who could not speak for themselves. He was the victim of his own outspoken boldness. He is dead, but his voice still speaks."

But when one such as Father Coughlin speaks on your behalf, beware. It turned out that Buckley was on the payroll of both Ford Motor Company and the Feds as a special investigator. While he may have been genuinely concerned about harm to the city's workers from mob-catered booze, gambling and other vices, he may also have been on the take. In fact, Detroit Police Commissioner Thomas Wilcox was adamant that Buckley was a known extortionist, and his death just another day in the life of a mobster.

According to a *Detroit News* story, Buckley's death had a positive effect on the city. "Shootings which had given 1930 the nickname 'Bloody Thirty' abruptly stopped. Gunmen, frightened by the city's wrath, fled as the clean-up, following Bowles' recall, delved into murky corners."

From Detroit to Your Living Room

The world's first news broadcast is believed to have originated from WWJ, owned by the Detroit News, on August 31, 1920. While only an estimated 30 households heard it, it helped boost radio into a profitable medium rather than just a nerd's hobby.

WXYZ radio, a CBS affiliate chartered in 1930, helped the country escape the ugliness of mob murders and the Great Depression by giving life to some of pop culture's most enduring crime fighters. It was a hard slog at first, as station owners tried to grasp the right formula to attract viewers and advertisers. They were hemorrhaging money, partly because they employed 65 musicians at a time when live music was a regular feature of many stations.

So station owner George Trendle hired Fran Striker, a writer from Buffalo, New York, and together they came up with that masked man, The Lone Ranger.

After the first few episodes aired locally, they decided to give him a sidekick, an American Indian named Tonto. That way, he wouldn't have to just talk to his horse Silver all the time. Tonto's introduction helped boost the show's popularity. Unfortunately, Tonto's clipped, two-word sentences and clothing that looked like it came from a souvenir shop also helped inform Hollywood's stereotypes of Native Americans. Kemosabe, Tonto's famous nickname for the Ranger, comes from Kamp Kee-Mo Sah-Bee on Mullett Lake near Cheboygan.

Most radio serials during the Depression were coming from New York and Los Angeles. Yet this straight-as-an-arrow Western hero, with white hat and black mask caught on, and was soon riding out of the industrial Midwest into millions of radios across the country.

By the end of the decade, the crew was doing three live performances, three nights a week, to accommodate different time zones. It got pretty cramped in there with actors, technicians and the sound effects people who re-created a horse's gallop by slapping rubber plungers into a tub of sand.

The live radio show rode on for 21 years, originating from the 14th floor of what is now called the Maccabees building. It currently houses Wayne State University offices, at 5057 Woodward Avenue. The show was on the leading edge of the Western film and TV genre, which was all the rage in the 1950s and into the 60s.

The station also started other dramas that — in today's lingo — went viral. The Green Hornet used pretty much the same formula as The Lone Ranger, right down to the minority sidekick. This time, it was in a more modern, urban setting. Also, The Challenge of the Yukon would later become Sergeant Preston of the Yukon.

WXYZ became an ABC affiliate in 1946, and has since morphed into Channel 7 on TV.

THOUSANDS THRONG STREETS AS JERRY BUCKLEY IS LAID TO REST

Detroit Free Press, July 27, 1930

MURDER MAP

The broadcast studio where Buckley railed against Mayor Bowles and organized criminals was located at the LaSalle Hotel on **2560 Woodward Avenue** at the corner of **Adelaide Street**. WMBC was changed to WJLB in 1939, under a new owner. JLB is now a hip-hop station.

The LaSalle lobby was also where Buckley met his end. He wasn't the only one. A week before Buckley's murder, two drug-peddlers were gunned down on the hotel's front steps, and a cigarette girl jumped — or was thrown — from the hotel's roof. The year before, John McLeod sued the hotel for negligence after someone threw his daughter through the open doors of a moving elevator, killing her.

Not surprisingly, LaSalle's history didn't exactly make it the most popular hotel destination — well, maybe for gawking, but not for a good night's rest. The hotel underwent several name changes over the next couple of decades, as well as several sweeping renovations. Still no luck. It later became a Catholic home for the elderly, but has since been torn down.

The site is now covered by condominiums neighboring Comerica Park, Ford Field and the Fox Theater, with the new Red Wings arena rising right across the street.

Corktown, where Buckley was reared, is the oldest Detroit neighborhood still in existence. A few blocks south of downtown, it's one of the rapidly gentrifying areas of the city. Many formerly blue-collar bars and restaurants have gone more upscale, for better or worse. Some industrial buildings, like an old The Grinnell Bros. piano factory from the early 20th Century, are being turned into toney loft apartments.

Corktown is bordered by the **Lodge Freeway** and **I-75**, and extends from the old Tiger Stadium site to the magnificent but vacant Michigan Central Station.

ST. VALENTINE'S DAY MASSACRE

THE YEAR: 1929
THE CRIME: MURDER
THE MOTIVE: HIJACKING THE HOOCH

CHICAGO'S ST. VALENTINE'S DAY MASSACRE IS THE MOST FAMOUS, OR INFAMOUS, PROHIBITION-ERA MOB SLAUGHTER.

Seven people — six associates of George "Bugs" Moran and a mechanic — were lined up against a garage wall and mowed down with Tommy guns.

No, Detroit's meanest didn't pull the triggers, but in theories and rumors, the Purples played a supporting role.

Purple brother Abe Bernstein is said to have called Bugs Moran the day before Valentine's Day, telling him a shipment of whiskey was on its way to the S.M.C. Cartage Co. garage. Bugs was disappointed at Capone's prices on quality hooch from Canada (courtesy of the Purples), and had decided to start intercepting the shipments. Hijacking, in other words, the trucks sent by the Purple Gang. The St. Valentine's Day Massacre may have been Capone's way of letting Bugs know he was on to him, and settling the score.

In fact, the hit may have been intended to take down Bugs himself. He was a cautious fellow, though, and late to the meeting. When one of his men saw two policemen approaching the garage, Bugs turned around and headed to a nearby coffee shop.

The cops, however, were impersonators — the whole shebang a setup, courtesy of Capone. The fake cops, along with two other guys in long overcoats, stormed into the garage where Moran's men waited for the booze. They lined them up and sprayed them full of lead. To finish off the charade, the two fake cops walked the long-coats out with their hands up.

But were the Purples involved? Police showed photos of Purple members to a landlady who'd rented rooms to three apparent lookouts for the hit. She identified them as Harry and Phil Keywell and Eddie Fletcher, all Purples.

The Purple Gang, incognito.

The abduction of aviation superstar Charles Lindbergh's 20-month-old son in 1932 in New Jersey was one of the most notorious cases of child murder before JonBenét Ramsey (a one-time Little Miss Charlevoix) was found dead in her parents Colorado home 64 years later.

Lindbergh was born in Detroit, and his mom taught chemistry at Detroit Cass Technical High School. A Detroit nurse may have aided and abetted the baby heist — she had a brother in the Purple Gang. The child was eventually found, dead, about four miles from his home.

The high-profile nature of the case led Congress to enact the "Lindbergh Law," making kidnapping a federal offense under some circumstances, like transporting the victim across state lines.

1929 Detroit skyline.

When in Rome

With three of every four bottles of illegal liquor in America flowing through the city, setting up a speakeasy was pretty much a no-brainer.

By 1925, there were at least 25,000 of them in greater Detroit. Gambling dens, opium parlors and brothels also sprang up, and you could get a drink there too.

The term "speakeasy" probably originated in the United States, but Brits may have invented it as code — "speak softly shop" — for where to get a cheap drink in the late 1900s. Blind pigs and blind tigers also made their appearance at that time. They were even more disreputable — a whole step down in class from a speakeasy.

Book-Cadillac Hotel

Although no massacres have taken place at the Book-Cadillac at 1114 Washington Boulevard, it is tragically famous in baseball lore. In 1939, Lou Gehrig fell down the hotel's grand staircase, and shortly thereafter, in one of the hotel's bars, told the Yankees manager that he was taking himself off the starting line-up. So on May 2, at Briggs Stadium (later Tiger Stadium), he ended his then-record streak of 2,130 consecutive games played and stepped off the bench to tip his hat to the wild applause.

He would later be diagnosed with ALS, now known as Lou Gehrig's disease.

The Book-Cadillac, these days a Westin, has hosted many celebrities over the years, including the Beatles, Elvis Presley, Frank Sinatra and Dr. Martin Luther King Jr. Other distinguished guests included presidents Franklin D. Roosevelt, John F. Kennedy, Harry S. Truman, Ronald Reagan and Herbert Hoover. The hotel was also the setting for Frank Capra's 1947 movie "State of the Union," starring Katharine Hepburn and Spencer Tracy.

The Purple Gang

Early Detroit gang wars started around 1910 when the Black Hand, a Sicilian import operating out of the Eastern Market, was threatened by a newbie group of expat mobsters. Between 1916 and 1919, over 100 men died. A truce was called on Thanksgiving in 1920, and Detroit was divided into east and west mob territories. Chester "Big Chet" LaMare (see next page) ruled the west from his Venice Café headquarters in Hamtramck. The Purple Gang controlled the Detroit River north and south of the city.

So what happened to the Purple Gang? The answer is, the better they dressed, the sloppier they became. Years of near impunity from the law made them rich and arrogant. They bought fine houses, dressed to the nines, and hung out at the best restaurants and night clubs. They also began to fight among themselves. In 1931, three Purple members who'd been making trouble (they'd developed their own liquor smuggling operation, called The Little Jewish Navy, using high-speed boats) were invited to a peace negotiation at the Collingwood Manor Apartment. Bang, bang, bang. Three other Purple members were found guilty of the murders, including founder Ray Bernstein. All three were sent to prison with life sentences. It's alleged, however, that Ray's brother Abe never gave it up, and continued to run a bookie operation out of his suite at the Book-Cadillac Hotel. He died of a stroke in 1968.

Power Through Intimidation

There are different ways to gain power. With the Purple Gang — and organized crime in general, as well as dictatorships and other bullying enterprises — it came from being scarier, more ruthless and more willing to kill than the next guy. The Purples graduated from street thuggery and carefully honed their reputations with murder and mayhem. On the other hand, if they could get what they wanted without killing — just by, say, scaring the living daylights out of someone — they often took that higher road.

Take the Cleaners and Dyers War. The gang was working with a local union to organize the industry and institute city-wide price fixing. Not all of the plant owners wanted to go along with it.

So imagine walking up the steps to open your business for the morning and finding a stick of dynamite with a half-burned wick. Dynamite can be a pretty convincing negotiating tool. The Purples also had a habit of showing up at union meetings visibly armed. Were you thinking about not handing over your dues to the nice man with the gun? Might wanna think again.

Businessmen who were difficult to persuade might get their plants bombed. Stink-bombing was a popular method of ruination, thus destroying the wares by making them smell like a rotting corpse. The Purples mixed it up, though, so the victim wouldn't know just what form the retaliation might take.

It got even more sinister and creative than that. Chemicals were sneaked onto clothing. When a worker pressed the clothing — Poof! — it burst into flames.

It was not murder, but extortion — the legal term for intimidation for gain — that brought the Purples to court and ended the Cleaners and Dyers War. But again, they were all acquitted when witnesses suddenly changed their minds about testifying. Was it a half-burnt dynamite wick or a dirty look from the defendants' table? Who knows?

KING OF HAMTRAMCK

THE YEAR: 1931
THE CRIME: MURDER
THE MOTIVE: POWER STRUGGLE

IN PROHIBITION-ERA MOB SPEAK, TO PUT SOMEONE "ON THE SPOT" WAS THE SAME AS ICING OR OFFING THEM.

The spot where that happened to mobster Chester "Big Chet" LaMare was the kitchen of his fortified home on Grandville Avenue, a comfortable neighborhood street on the west side. He was shot six hours before he was to be arrested and brought before a grand jury.

Chester LaMare was born in Sicily, the fourth of twelve children. These were high times for Sicilians to leave their Mediterranean island, as economic and political strife were hitting it hard. LaMare joined the exodus and arrived in the United States in 1902. He did a bit of this and that in Manhattan, and then Chicago, before arriving in Detroit in 1918.

But the Motor City crime scene was no place for newcomers. He worked as a hired gun for the Gianolla brothers, ordering drive-by shootings — a practice that was gangster before it was gangsta — and inspiring gambling bookies to do business with him by dipping them in the cold Detroit River. But LaMare longed to be a boss. He got his chance when a pal of his, John Vitale, split to form his own gang. A year later, the Gianollas were dead, and LaMare was named king of Hamtramck.

In those days, Hamtramck was a boom town. The Dodge brothers had opened a plant there in 1914, and thousands of Europeans, particularly Poles, arrived to build the future. LaMare set about building his own boomtown of brothels, gambling houses and speakeasies. He headquartered his operation in a nightspot called the Venice Café. Of course, any neighboring businesses had to pay LaMare…or else.

But he gave back too, to the politicians and the police. Alas, Hamtramck became so notorious for corruption that Michigan Governor Alex Groesbeck finally had to send in the State Police. In 1922, the doors to the Venice Café were chained shut. Thirty-one men were prosecuted, including Hamtramck's mayor.

But not LaMare. It took four years to get him into court, and then he managed to walk out with probation. He was, by all accounts, a charming fellow in the right company.

The year 1929 found LaMare scrambling to take control of the east side mob while ducking in and out of Detroit. He was also ducking grand jury indictments. On February 6, 1930, police had secured an arrest warrant and were planning to raid LaMare's home. Two fellow mobsters got to him first. Invited into the kitchen for a midnight chat, one of them stood up behind him and put a hole in his head.

It was clear right away that LaMare was "put on the spot" by someone he'd known and trusted. There was no break-in, and he was killed in the only room where he didn't keep a loaded weapon. His wife was initially suspected of the killing, and she may have helped.

Police found quite the arsenal in the LaMare home: pistols, rifles, 2,500 rounds of ammo, a gas grenade and a James Bond-ish fountain-pen gas gun. He and his wife slept with loaded pistols under their pillows.

MACKLIN REMANDED FOR MURDER. Elmer Macklin, charged with the murder of Chester LaMare, Wednesday, was ordered held without bail at his examination before Judge John P. Scallen in the Recorder's Court. Mrs. Anna LaMare, widow of the slain gang leader, testified, but failed to accuse Macklin.

Detroit Free Press, October 15, 1931

Luckiest Man
• • • • • • • • • • • • •

At the time of his death, and besides his mobster gig, LaMare also had a job at an auto plant, which allowed him to pose as just another Detroit working stiff. It wasn't that simple. Harry Bennett, the unofficial security adviser for the Ford Motor Company, had specifically hired LaMare to keep the peace with the Italian workforce. As further incentive, Bennett gave LaMare the Crescent Motor Sales Company and a fruit concession at Ford's River Rouge Plant. Both were so-called licenses to print money. In 1928, LaMare's net worth was estimated at $215 million, equivalent to almost $3 billion today.

When troubles arrived in the form of the Governor, these legitimate businesses helped get him off the hook with a fine. His association with the Secret Service as a confidential informant didn't hurt either.

MURDER MAP

Chester LaMare's home is at **15505 Grandville**, a block south of **Grand River Avenue**. From the outside, it still looks about like it did in the news photos from more than 85 years ago.

A Detroit distillery flushed by police.

Crossing the Detroit River with sleds.

TREACHERY ON THE INLAND SEAS

THE YEAR: 1900s – 1930s
THE CRIME: MURDER
THE MOTIVE: THE RICHES OF THE NON-BRINY

DAN SEAVEY WAS A LOT OF THINGS.

He was a sailor, a Navy veteran, a businessman, an intense and vicious fighter, a con man, a kidnapper and pimp, a bootlegger and a killer. He's best known as the Great Lakes pirate, "Roaring Dan."

Seavey didn't look anything like Blackbeard or Jack Sparrow. His dapper appearance was more 20th century. Pictures show a guy wearing a dark suit, under a modest, billed sailor's cap, with eyes that could size up friend or foe in no time.

He left home in Maine at 13 to work on merchant ships. After a stint in the U.S. Navy, he moved to Marinette, Wisconsin, got married, fathered a daughter and started a farm. Later, he moved the family to Milwaukee and added saloon-keep to his resume. But he bolted his family and everything else in 1898 to seek his fortune in the Klondike Gold Rush. Two years later, broke and disappointed, he returned to the western shore of Lake Michigan. And that's when the pirating began.

Seavey got ahold of a schooner, the *Wanderer*, and started a shipping company in Escanaba. Legitimate cargo filled his hold some of the time. But why take an inch when you can sail a mile? Sneaking around the docks of a port town at night, he looked for unguarded freight — be it venison, cattle, booze or lumber. Other times, he disabled or altered navigational buoys causing ships to run aground. Then, he and his crew hopped on board and loaded as much of its goods as they could onto the *Wanderer*.

Seavey has been romanticized in some Great Lakes lore, but to do so is to ignore some of his most vile exploits. For one, he is said to have kidnapped frontier women and sold them into prostitution. He made money during the transport by inviting male customers aboard.

And what pirate story would be complete without a cannon? When a company by the name of Booth Fisheries ignored his orders to stop horning in on his illegal venison trade, he put a cannon on the deck. A shot at Booth's boat blew a hole in it and the entire crew was killed.

One of his most famous crimes was the 1908 hijacking, in Charlevoix, of the *Nellie Johnson*. Seavey first befriended the crew with a big jug of liquor. Then, he pretended to keep up as the captain and crew went from buzzed to blitzed. In no time, they were sloshing around the deck with slurry renditions of "did I ever tell you you're a great guy…." and falling down. That was Mission Accomplished for Roaring Dan. He tossed the captain overboard, in chains, and sailed to Chicago.

After taking his profits from the sale of the ship and its valuable cargo of cedar logs, Seavey hopped back aboard the *Wanderer*.

This time the law followed. Federal revenue officers pursued him for days. They finally caught up with him and returned him in chains, but alive, to Chicago on charges of ship-napping. Alas, when the *Nellie Johnson* could not be found, and no one was around to dispute Seavey's claim that the captain had given him the ship, there was nothing to do but let him go.

In later life, Roaring Dan is said to have quit pirating to help federal officers keep scoundrels like himself off the Great Lakes.

On the other hand, just as Prohibition was getting started, he purchased a 40-foot motor boat — the perfect vehicle for smuggling hooch.

MURDER MAP

Lake Michigan, the only one of the five Great Lakes that the U.S. does not share with Canada, is where Roaring Dan Seavey did his worst. If you're fortunate enough to own a boat, you could see the many picturesque lakefront towns just how Seavey did, by sailing into port. A Dan Seavey tour would have to include Milwaukee, Wisconsin, where he once lived; Escanaba, Michigan, his home-base in pirating days; and Chicago, Illinois, where he'd convert stolen and otherwise illegal goods into cash.

Also, the resort town of Charlevoix is where he stole the Nellie Johnson. He's also known to have sailed into Frankfort, Ludington, and Grand Haven, among others. He even stopped in Fayette on occasion. At that time, the Upper Peninsula settlement was emptying out after a quarter-century run as an iron-smelting company town. Now, it's a well-preserved ghost town with historical exhibits and a Michigan state park.

RUNNING ON EMPTY

THE YEAR: 1982
THE CRIME: MURDER
THE MOTIVE: HATE

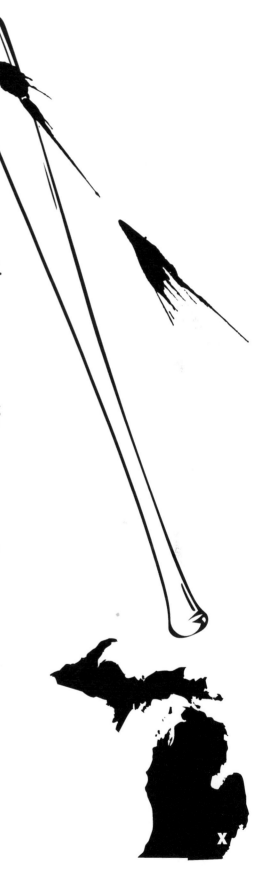

IT WAS 1982 AND JAPANESE CAR COMPANIES WERE WAGING THE FIRST SERIOUS CHALLENGE TO DETROIT'S DOMINANCE IN THE AMERICAN MARKET.

Throughout the 70s, Detroit's focus had been big cars, big trucks, big gas guzzlers. But oil shortages in '73 and '79 made economy-sized vehicles attractive to many Americans. Japan jumped to supply them.

By 1980, more than 100,000 American-brand auto-workers had lost their jobs, and Japan had nearly 30% of the market.

Needless to say, there was a bit of anti-Japanese venom going around. Datsuns and Toyotas were dismissed as "rice burners," Pearl Harbor would get brought up, the f-bombs would fly. Add a major recession to the mix and you've got a recipe for violence.

On June 19, Vincent Chin was the guest of honor for his own bachelor party at a now-defunct all-nude strip club, Fancy Pants, on Woodward in Highland Park. Also in the club were laid-off Chrysler plant supervisor Ronald Ebens and his equally laid-off stepson, Michael Nitz. You can't blame alcohol for what followed as, under Michigan law, clubs with all-nude dancers don't get to serve booze like topless joints do.

Ebens started it by yelling at Chin and his friends, saying they were responsible for Detroit's dire straits. Although Chin was Chinese, to embittered Ebens, Japan and China were like apples and apples.

More racial insults and taunts were hurled, peppered with those f-bombs, and Chin seemed more than happy to take the bait. Finally, the bouncers told them to move it outside. Chin and Ebens almost got into it on the sidewalk, but the groom's friends broke it up and scooted him away.

Ebens was boiling. He wasn't going to let it go. He opened the trunk of his car and grabbed the Louisville Slugger baseball bat he kept there. Then, father and son searched the nearby blocks for two hours, even paying a guy $20 to help. When they finally spotted Chin under the golden arches of a McDonald's, Nitz ran up and held him as his stepfather beat the 27-year-old senseless with the bat.

Chin never made it to his wedding. He died a few days later, having never recovered consciousness.

The father-son team were initially charged with murder, but plea-bargained down to manslaughter. Wayne County Judge Charles Kaufman softened that blow even further by only sentencing them with probation and fines. Michigan Congressman John Conyers, Jr. said the light sentences resulted because the case was a "hot potato" and untouchable for "political reasons" that could be damaging to the automobile industry.

Asian Americans throughout the country were outraged, and appealed for justice. Chin's murder became a touchstone in the drive to establish hate crime laws, as well as uniting the political activism of different nationalities of Asians.

Chin's family did successfully sue the men for wrongful death.

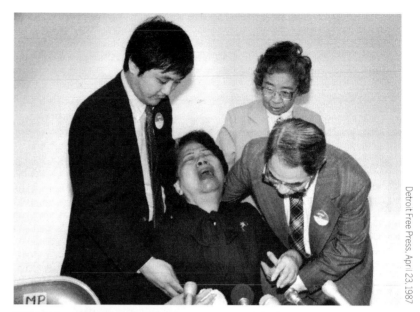

Detroit Free Press, April 23, 1987

Lily Chin, Vincent's mother, collapses after retelling the story of her son's death.

Hate Crimes
• • • • • • • • • • • •

Forty-five states and the District of Columbia now have statutes criminalizing various types of hate crimes. The exceptions are Arkansas, Georgia, Indiana, South Carolina and Wyoming. Michigan is one of only two states that recognize sexual orientation for hate crime data collection.

MURDER MAP

The strip club was located in the old Highland Park Theater at **13843 Woodward**. It was built in 1915, 12 years before movies had sound. It later became the Hiland and then, when suburban multiplexes were decimating the smaller, neighborhood theaters, it turned into Fancy Pants.

The modest and now boarded-up theater is across the street from the building that put the American middle class on wheels. The Ford Model T plant was built seven years earlier than the movie house. It would have been in full swing for assembly line workers who wanted to catch the latest Charlie Chaplin movies.

HIPPIE HATERS GONNA HATE

THE YEAR: 1970
THE CRIME: MURDER
THE MOTIVE: GENERATION GAP

ARVILLE GARLAND DROVE A TRAIN FOR A LIVING AND RAISED HIS FAMILY IN A WORKING CLASS NEIGHBORHOOD WITHIN WALKING DISTANCE OF A MAJOR NETWORK OF RAIL-YARDS.

His daughter, Sandra, seemed to be the fulfillment of every parent's dream: first a model high school student, then pre-med at Wayne State. But Sandra's choice of friends — black — and her housing arrangement — a commune — sent the dream off the rails.

It was the Age of Aquarius. Although Rowan & Martin's Laugh-In helped popularize the hippie movement, 1970 was long before hacky sacks and the passage of time had softened the image. Most parents still feared that sex, drugs and rock-n-roll would turn their children into deranged freeloaders. Unable to reason with his daughter, Arville took matters into his own hands.

At 2 in the morning on May 8, 1970, Arville busted into Stonehead Manor with a Luger and a .38 automatic. He claimed he'd carried a pistol in each hand in case anyone resisted his efforts to grab his 17-year-old daughter and bring her home. No one did. They were all asleep. Arville said the first shot went off by accident, hitting Sandra. Then he went crazy, pumping several more slugs into his daughter, as well as three of her friends who happened to be sleeping — in separate sleeping bags — in the same room. Unable to find his daughter's roommate, he stopped to reload and drove a few more into Sandra.

Incredibly, his wife Martha was waiting outside during the mayhem — although she thought they were only there to bring their daughter home. The gunshots alerted her to her error and she forced her husband to not only leave the building, but to turn himself in to the police. Arville calmly walked over to the Detroit Police precinct office on Vernor, handed over his guns and confessed to the officer on duty.

Free Press Photo by JOE LIPPINCOTT

SANDRA'S father, Arville Garland, is led to Recorder's Court Friday by Detective Sgt. Irvin Boranski.

Detroit Free Press, May 9, 1970

Hey Joe
• • • • • • • •

Two months after the murders, the movie "Joe" hit theaters, starring the late Peter Boyle (remember Ray's dad on Everybody Loves Raymond?). In the movie, Joe helps another guy search for his daughter. FORTY-FIVE-YEAR-OLD SPOILER ALERT: When they find her living in a commune, they shoot up the place, killing a bunch of hippies. Boyle was sickened when he witnessed theater audiences cheering the violence.

Interestingly, the judge in Arville Garland's trial advised lawyers on both sides to see the movie, then tried to only seat jurors who had not seen it.

"I want to turn myself in," he said.

"For what?" asked the officer.

"For murder. I just murdered my daughter and her hippie friends."

Except that he didn't actually consider it murder, and certainly not a crime. Arville was quoted at the time to say, "She's my daughter and I can do whatever I want with her." The police let him go home.

During the extremely well publicized trial, hundreds of people wrote Arville admiring letters of support. The judge sympathized. Orville got off with ten years.

Coincidentally, the massacre at Stonehead Manor took place only three days after National Guard troops killed four protesting Kent State University students in Ohio. Both tragedies came to symbolize the enormous chasm between generations: obedience to authority and tradition on one side, anti-war protests and experimentation with sex and drugs on the other.

MURDER MAP

Stonehead Manor stood at **4330 Lincoln Street**, near the Wayne State University campus. That spot is now an unmarked, unimproved vacant lot among mostly well-kept townhouses a few blocks north of the MotorCity Casino Hotel.

Sandra Garland graduated in 1969 from Chadsey High School at **5335 Martin Street**. The school was built in 1931 and demolished in 2011.

Sandra had lived with her family at **5755 Otis** on the city's near-west side. A home still stands there in the working class neighborhood, presumably the one in which she grew up.

Mexicantown is a few blocks southeast of the old Garland home, in the heart of the heavy industry and working class neighborhoods between old Tiger Stadium and Dearborn.

RIDING WITH A KILLER

THE YEAR: 2016
THE CRIME: MURDER
THE MOTIVE: UNKNOWN

JASON DALTON WAS AN UBER DRIVER.

Uber is a digital-age take on the taxi cab — in which people summon a ride with a phone app. The drivers use their own cars and offer rides when they want, where they want. No old-fashioned cash changes hands, just electronic transactions.

The concept was gaining a lot of attention in early 2016, as part of the newly formed "sharing economy." Then Jason Dalton shot his way onto the scene and gave post-9/11 Americans one more thing to fear.

It was a Saturday night in Kalamazoo, and Dalton was on the job. Usually friendly and jovial (so said people who knew him), he'd become depressed lately. In fact, his wife had just filed for divorce. And early that evening he received an upsetting phone call. The customer in his car could tell he was agitated, later saying that he was running stop signs and just generally driving badly. The rider couldn't wait to get out, jumping from the car a block before his destination.

Later, after dropping a female passenger at her home, Dalton started the spree. He took out the 9mm handgun he'd had hidden in the car and shot and wounded a woman outside an apartment complex. Back to work.

As he zoomed around the freeways and cloverleafs skirting the city, he continued to pick up unsuspecting riders. Between fares, he approached unsuspecting strangers with his gun, police say. He walked up and shot a man and his son as they browsed through a Kia car dealer's lot. The 17-year-old son's girlfriend watched them die from the backseat of a parked car. Later in the evening, Dalton went to the parking lot of a Cracker Barrel restaurant and killed four women sitting in cars. A 14-year-old girl was also injured.

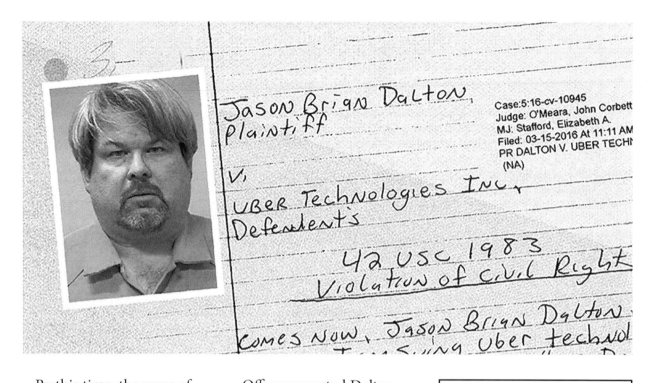

Jason Brian Dalton,
Plaintiff

V.

Uber Technologies Inc,
Defendents

Case:5:16-cv-10945
Judge: O'Meara, John Corbett
MJ: Stafford, Elizabeth A.
Filed: 03-15-2016 At 11:11 AM
PR DALTON V. UBER TECH'
(NA)

42 USC 1983
Violation of civil Right

Comes Now, Jason Brian Dalton
suing Uber technol

By this time, the news of an Uber killer had hit the media, and authorities were warning of a sniper on the loose. One man visiting from Indianapolis took an Uber ride because he didn't want to walk around with a shooter still out there. Dalton ended up being his Uber man.

The man told a local TV station, "I kind of jokingly said to the driver, 'You're not the shooter, are you?' He gave me some sort of a 'no' response...shook his head."

"I said, 'Are you sure?' And he said, 'No, I'm not, I'm just tired.' And we proceeded to have a pretty normal conversation after that."

Officers arrested Dalton later that night. According to the *Detroit Free Press*, n police interviews Dalton said a devil's head came out of the Uber app, told him to shoot people and took over his body.

He's charged with six counts of murder and is headed to trial.

MURDER MAP

Seelye Kia is on **Stadium Drive** near Western Michigan University campus, and the Cracker Barrel is on the southwest side of the city.

Kalamazoo appears in more than a dozen popular songs, due to the lyricism of its name — just as good as Timbuktu. In the past, it was also the location of many tabloid-reported, posthumous Elvis Presley sightings.

BEWARE THE BLUE GREMLIN

THE YEAR: 1976 – 1977
THE CRIME: MURDER
THE MOTIVE: UNSPEAKABLE

IN 1976 AND '77, SOMEONE KIDNAPPED AND KILLED FOUR PRE-TEENS IN THE NORTHERN DETROIT SUBURBS — TWO BOYS AND TWO GIRLS — AND LEFT THEM IN SNOWBANKS OR DITCHES.

After the third victim, ten-year-old Kristine Mihelich, disappeared on January 2, 1977, the murder investigation became the most extensive, at that point, in U.S. history. But nobody was ever arrested, and the fear and paranoia felt by metro Detroit parents lingered for years.

In the decades since, the case has grown old but not cold. Even now, 40 years later, new leads, theories and suspects continue to surface.

Perhaps the most famous of the clues was the blue AMC Gremlin. Early on, the police told a public hungry for answers that the killer may have been driving the economy hatchback when he abducted his victims. People began noticing the small cars with suspicions far beyond the usual, "Why would anyone buy such an ugly car?" Every single Gremlin owner in Oakland County was interviewed. These days, however, investigators say the Gremlin was a red-herring. Kind of late for all of the guys who endured endless suspicion based on their cars and have long since gotten rid of them.

Then came reports that the killer may be someone who died in a car crash in Wyoming. In 1999, the prosecutor and forensics scientists flew out West to exhume the body and take a DNA sample. It didn't match.

Similarly, John Wayne Gacy, the serial killer and rapist from Cook County, Illinois, who did more to damage to the image of clowns than anyone in history, was a suspect. DNA testing did not find a match there either.

SHERIFF'S DEPT
PONTIAC MICH
56982

POLICE DEPT.
DES PLAINES, ILL.
78-462.12-21-78

Busch and Gacy.

In the mid-70s, Gacy invented two clown characters, "Pogo the Clown" and "Patches the Clown." He regularly performed at children's parties, parades, and fundraising events.

Barry King, the father of the last of the four victims, has another theory. He believes Christopher Busch, a convicted pedophile who copped a plea deal in another case and committed suicide in his parents' Bloomfield Township home in 1978, may be the killer. He claims investigators agreed to kick the suspicions under the rug because his father was a powerful General Motors executive. King, an attorney, has unsuccessfully sued for the release of all investigative records.

The most scientific link, however, came in 2012. A hair found on Kristine Mihelich matched a man named James Gunnels. Coincidentally, perhaps, as a teenager, Gunnels had been molested by Christopher Busch, for which Busch was convicted.

Whoever the killer was, the spree thankfully ended after the fourth child showed up dead and discarded in a ditch off 8 Mile Road in Livonia. Still, the public would rather have seen it resolved.

MURDER MAP

Oakland County is a symbol of white affluence in the Detroit area, as the inner city has long been a symbol of black poverty. The road that divides them, **8 Mile**, is likewise an icon of that division. Oakland to the north, Detroit and Wayne County to the south. Of course, the road lent its name and significance to white Detroit rapper Eminem's semi-autobiographical movie. Longtime Detroit Mayor Coleman Young also seized on the division in one of his most famous quotes about crime:

> "I issue a warning to all those pushers, to all rip-off artists, to all muggers: It's time to leave Detroit; hit 8 Mile Road! And I don't give a damn if they are black or white, or if they wear Superfly suits or blue uniforms with silver badges. Hit the road."

If you cross **8 Mile** on, say, **Woodward** or **Livernois** avenues, the contrast is noticeable, though nothing like the blink-of-an-eye transformation between the city and Grosse Pointe on **Jefferson Avenue**.

Oakland County has many small lakes and upscale cities of different flavors. There are the surging art scenes of Royal Oak and Ferndale, and the exclusive bedroom communities of Birmingham and Bloomfield Hills.

The county seat is Pontiac, which stands in contrast to the county and its reputation, with larger minority populations and lower household incomes.

next recall of that situation was that her father was somehow
discussing what to do with the boy's body.

then explained that she witnessed a second
homicide of a nine year old female whom she cannot identify.
stated that she was approximately 12 years old at the time
of this death.   does not recall where the death took place
or who took the girl's life.   could only remember that she
was in an office which to her at the time appeared to be a
doctor's office and that a girl approximately nine years old was
lying naked on an examining table. The girl had long dark brown
hair. The girl appeared to be, in   words, pre-pubescent.
stated that she witnessed the girl being sexually abused
and becoming very frenzied regarding this treatment, as a result
of an individual began to what appeared to be stabbing the girl
in the stomach and then she remembers the girl falling off the
table and lying on the ground in an awkward angle.   then
remembers that there was some discussion as to what would be done
with this girl.

stated that she believes her father was involved
at the time in a pedophile or child abuser's ring. She stated
that her father recruited members for this ring from his
associates and from members of ST. JOSEPH'S CHURCH which is
located in Dexter, Michigan. She stated that at the time her
father was employed at   as a
in Ann Arbor, Michigan.   further stated that there was an
individual whom she cannot identify residing in Ann Arbor who was
the ring leader for this particular organization of people. She
stated that the only thing she can recall is that he was a very
prominent and powerful person in the Ann Arbor community. She
stated that he was a very large man with dark hair and possibly a
beard.   also advised that   date
of birth   , telephone number   also
molested her and had sexual intercourse with her up until she was
18 years of age. She stated that there was also an individual
identified as   who owned and operated a practice on Main
        n in Dexter, Michigan. According to
        performed an abortion on her sister,   who was
pregnant with their father's child.   stated that her
father forced her to watch this abortion with the plan that if
        was sufficiently shocked at this situation she would not
become pregnant.

One of the documents provided by the Michigan State Police in response to Barry King's FOIA request for files relating to the investigation of Frank Shelden and allegations concerning North Fox Island.

Stranger Danger

The Oakland County Killer set off a panic in southeastern Michigan. Parents refused to let their children walk to school, playgrounds were abandoned, and children were repeatedly advised to never, ever talk to strangers.

The fact of the matter is that only 10% of violent crimes toward children involve strangers, and the percentage is even lower for sex offenses.

North Fox Island

Some believe a ring of pedophiles may have been responsible for the Oakland child killings. Real estate magnate Francis Shelden owned North Fox, an island near the tip of Leelanau county. In the 1970s, Shelden had an airstrip built so that he could easily fly his plane there from Ann Arbor. At that time, Shelden was in his forties, rich, well-educated and a man who liked to give money to "help" boys. He and some other associates started a "nature camp" called Brother Paul's Children's Mission on the island. However, two boys from Benton Harbor came forward with tales of molestation. Photos were found in child porn magazines that seemed to substantiate the claims. In 1976, the chief organizer of Brother Paul's was arrested on criminal charges of sexual molestation of a minor. When a warrant was signed for Shelden's arrest, he disappeared, setting off an international manhunt. He was never brought back to the United States and died in the Netherlands in 1996.

The State of Michigan purchased North Fox Island in 2000 for 2.2 million dollars.

A WRONG TO FIND WRIGHT

THE YEAR: 1889
THE CRIME: MURDER
THE MOTIVE: TAXES

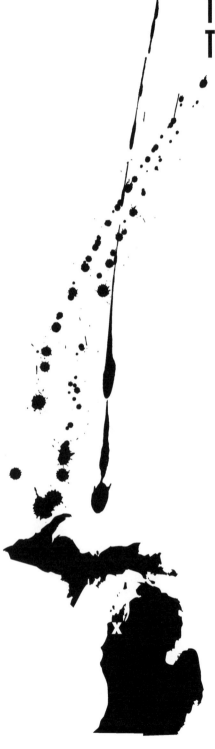

HERE'S A STORY THAT'S MORE FAMOUS FOR ITS CASE OF POLICE BRUTALITY THAN IT IS FOR THE MURDER ITSELF.

The incident took place in the sawmill town of Aral, population about 200, a few miles south of Empire. Don't look for it on a map — it only existed for a few decades, when the lumber boom was sweeping the trees from the northern lower peninsula. Perfectly situated for receiving timber, Aral boasted a decent creek for floating logs from inland, a millpond and access to Lake Michigan. When our story begins, it also had a post office, a couple of boarding houses for lumberjacks, horse barns, a school, a church, a meeting hall, a general store and a doctor. And it had a sawmill, operated by Charlie Wright.

Now Charlie Wright was a bit of a Jekyll-Hyde character. People liked him when he was sober, but drunk, he was stinking mean. And he was never meaner than the day the sheriff of Benzie County sent a deputy to discuss a tax dispute.

The deputy didn't get anything but threats from old Charlie Wright, so he headed into town for some back-up and returned with the doctor. Wright wasted no time. He shot them both, left them where they fell and went back to work

It wasn't long before word got out. Wright realized the town was talking about him and getting pretty worked up. Figuring they might be in the mood for some vigilante justice, he shut down the mill, paid off his workers and ran away into the woods.

But the sheriff was on his way, riding by buggy from Benzonia, then hitching a steamer from Frankfort to Aral. And he meant business. He traveled with a posse of twenty and went straight for the jugular, capturing Wright's right-hand man, a local Odawa man named Lahala.

The sheriff was sure Lahala knew where his boss had scampered to, but he wasn't talking. The sheriff had a solution.

He tossed a rope over a tree, hoisted the man into the air by the neck and told him to kick his legs when he was ready to talk.

It's not clear how one avoids kicking one's legs when dangling by a noose, but it wasn't long before Lahala was kicking madly.

This went on, the hoisting and the dropping of the blue-faced Odawa, until the words the sheriff knew were there gasped out. Wright was found and Lahala was released.

Wright went to the pen in Jackson, but later had his sentence commuted by Governor Hazen S. Pingree, who declared that politics had interfered with justice. The first thing Wright did was hightail it back to Aral, where his wife — who'd divorced him during his absence — lived with another man. Wright must have been persuasive, as she took him back, murder notwithstanding.

Mid-18th century sketch of an Odawa family by British soldier George Townshend.

A northern Michigan Odawa family from the 1800s.

MURDER MAP

It's been said that the hanging tree is still there — just off the dirt road that crosses Otter Creek at the south of **Esch Road**. Some also say it's obvious which of the trees is the hanging tree. But there are a lot of trees around there that look like they could support a noose, although trees obviously change a lot in 127 years.

There are also supposedly some building foundations still in the woods on the north side of **Esch Road**. The weather extremes on the sandy shores of Lake Michigan took care of the rest of the buildings over the century since the town ceased to exist.

In looking for the hanging tree, however, one may notice that it's next to one of the most beautiful beaches imaginable.

Otter Creek Beach is a spacious, sandy span on Lake Michigan which stretches for miles, offering a view of the rising Sleeping Bear Dunes to the north and stunning sunsets over the lake. Even if there's a lineup of cars on the pock-marked road, take heart. It's easy to get out of earshot — and sometimes eye-shot — of the other bathers. There are small dunes rolling all along the shorelines for added privacy.

There have long been rumors of people using Otter Creek as a nude beach at this or that point. Every now and then, someone gets arrested for indecent exposure, so it's good to make sure you're really alone when wearing nothing but an SPF 40.

Hermansville logging (above) and a rather decent camp company (below).

Interlochen without the trees.

Where Was the Epicenter of Michigan Logging?

That was a title that moved several times as the tree line receded. Saginaw, Seney, Menominee and others took their turns as the brawling, cussing, spitting hub of a rapacious industry.

Some of the old boom-towns don't even exist anymore. Walton Junction, between Kingsley and Fife Lake, is a quiet row of mid-century homes — nothing like the whiskey-soaked funland it was when poisoner Mary McKnight was arrested on the railroad platform while hoping to flee to Traverse City (see page 63).

Lumberjacks usually moved with the industry, wherever they were hiring. The towns that sprouted up around hiring supervisors generally reflected the industry's wandering ways. Saloons and brothels were meant to tempt the workers out of their hard-earned pay rather than set them up for a nice life with the wife and kids. As soon as the last white pines shipped out, so did the businesses.

These lumberjack transients were nothing like the Disney Paul Bunyans in popular culture or the plaid-clad lad on the Brawny paper towel packages.

The Ludington Record of October 6, 1881, describes them unattractively as "Frenchmen, Indians and half-breeds." Paul Bunyan lore — the giant who created lakes with his footsteps and had a gigantic pet blue ox — stems from stories the guys used to tell in the bunks. The ones we hear are pretty G-rated. One would expect that the originals were a bit less tame, as they were told by a bunch of those brawny misfits who might have gotten a hot bath once every spring, whether they needed it or not.

AND THE CROWD GOES CRAZY

THE YEAR: 1880
THE CRIME: MURDER
THE MOTIVE: IMMEDIATE JUSTICE

THE MCDONALD COUSINS WERE BAD NEWS.

They drank, whored and fought their way through the streets of Menominee, back when the town on the Wisconsin state line claimed to be the busiest lumber port in the world.

The cousins from Ontario must have really been something to stand out in a lumber camp. But such as it was, the supervisor at Quinnesec, on the Pine River, threw up his hands and called the sheriff.

The arrest — if it was an arrest, it might just have been a "talking to" — turned into a brawl. Frank McDonald, the younger of the two, beat the sheriff unconscious. The sheriff's burly deputy, George Kittson, took that matter in hand. He went up to the camp and arrested them both. A judge sent them to Jackson State Prison for a year and a half.

When that was over, the cousins went straight back to Menominee and started hitting the bars and brothels again. But now they were out for revenge, too.

Their first stop was the Montreal Boarding House in Menominee's Frenchtown. Deputy Kittson's brother was tending bar there, and the McDonalds started bragging about how they were going to pay his brother back.

From there, they strode on over to the Three Chimney House bordello, where they found another Kittson brother drinking whiskey with some of the women. You know about that attraction women have for bad boys? Apparently, the McDonald cousins were seriously bad, and the women stopped paying attention to Billy Kittson as soon as the McDonalds walked in. Pissed in more ways than one, Kittson broke a bottle over Frank McDonald's head and ran.

The McDonalds were hot on his heels, though. Armed with a lumberjack's hook, known as a Peavey, they overtook him, knocked him down, and stabbed him.

Here comes the bartender brother. In the ensuing brawl, young Frank McDonald got shot in the leg and Billy Kittson got stabbed again. When the bartender brother was fatally sliced with a knife in the face, that was the end of the Kittsons.

But not the McDonalds. Not yet. They got to a doctor, then high-tailed it out of town. The Menominee sheriff — a new one, not the old one whom they had beaten up before — arrested them and locked them in jail.

They never made it to court.

An angry mob of over 500 gathered outside the jail house. Using a telegraph pole, sledge-hammers and axes, they broke into the jail and dragged the cousins out, punching and pushing and kicking. They even knocked down a priest who tried to stop them.

Long ropes were tied around their necks, then fastened to a carriage. The driver snapped the reins and down Ogden Street they went, back to the brothel where the women liked "bad." It's not clear when the cousins died, but probably before the crowd strung them up a tree by their necks.

Yet it still wasn't over. The bodies were taken down, stomped on, then dragged inside the Three Chimney House bordello, where those Kittson-snubbing women were forced to lie with the corpses while the crowd laughed.

The mob ended up torching the brothel and stringing the McDonalds up again, where they hung, unmolested, for a few days.

Many in town were disgusted by the mob justice, but nobody was ever convicted.

MURDER MAP

Menominee, overlooking Green Bay — the bay, not the city — across the Menominee River from its twin city Marinette, Wisconsin. The name Menominee was also the name of an Indian tribe and means wild rice, a staple of the tribe's diet.

Quinnesec is up the Menominee River, which took the logs from here to Green Bay — still talking about the bay — and is over an hour's drive today.

DUNN IN

THE YEAR: 1880
THE CRIME: MURDER
THE MOTIVE: HE KILLED MY BROTHER

MICHIGAN HAD SEVERAL TOUGH BUT TEMPORARY LUMBERING TOWNS AS THE WHITE PINE BOOM SWEPT THROUGH THE STATE AND CHANGED THE LANDSCAPE FOREVER.

Seney, in the center of the U.P., was one of the roughest. It attracted hundreds of hard-drinking, fist-fighting lumbermen and tobacco-chewing saloon girls for the 15 or so years that the trees lasted.

But none of the cursing, brawling lumbermen could hold a kerosene lantern to Daniel Dunn, who owned one of the several saloons in town.

Dunn — spelled Dunne in some sources — actually started his notorious career in Roscommon, in the north-central Lower Peninsula. The allure of Seney's thirst must have called to him. But first, he needed money. Dunn hired a lumberman to burn down the saloon and brothel businesses he wanted to leave behind to move further north. Fifty bucks for the arsonist, the insurance for Dunn.

Off to Seney he went, quickly establishing a saloon to compete with the 20 or so other taverns (plus three brothels) already there.

Unfinished business from Roscommon soon came calling. A druggist, who'd loaned Dunn money, made the long trip up north to collect. Well, says Dunn, he doesn't quite have the cash, but he's working on it. He does, however, know of an ore deposit in a nearby bog. But shhh! "Promise to not tell anyone and I'll show it to you," he confides.

Out they went to the bog, and as the druggist was bending over to take a look at some of the "valuable" metal, Dunn shot him in the back of the head.

A little while later, another old Roscommon friend came calling. It happened to be the chap who'd burned down the brothel as a favor for Mr. Dunn. He wasn't doing so well, and decided that Dunn hadn't paid him quite enough. Let's just say he got to go look at the ore deposits in the bog, too.

There were mumblings around town about Dunn and his disappearing friends from downstate. But the one who finally said something about it to his face was Steve Harcourt. He was one of six Harcourt brothers, proprietors of a competing saloon/bordello, with no love for Daniel Dunn. Harcourt slipped into Dunn's business to talk trash and spit some accusations.

Dunn quickly had enough and broke a whiskey bottle over Harcourt's head, then shot him twice. Harcourt died a few days later, and Daniel Dunn was arrested for manslaughter. But the judge dismissed the charges — Dunn had acted in self-defense, the judge said.

Still, Dunn knew there were five more Harcourt brothers who would be seeking revenge. He thought if he could get to St. Ignace, he could get a court order to keep the brothers away. He took his wife along for the ride, and on the way they stopped at Trout Lake and got a room. He shouldn't have stopped. While looking out of his second floor digs, Dunn caught sight of brother Jim Harcourt. Dunn drew his pistol and sneaked down the stairs to take care of the threat, but Harcourt was ready for him and shot him four times.

After serving three years in Marquette State Prison, Jim Harcourt returned to Seney, a hero.

MURDER MAP

There's little sign of the lumber boom left in Seney. But if you are there, you may want to check out the Seney Wildlife Refuge, where you can often see nesting eagles. Munising and Pictured Rocks are to the west.

South of Seney is Blaney Park, a charming resort community that includes a restaurant and a general store, as well as rows of houses built in the 1920s by a lumber company looking for new income after the trees were felled. People periodically move in to get one of the business concerns or a B&B going. They don't always last, so there may or may not be much going on at the time you happen by. It's always worth a look.

Trout Lake has some businesses with a definite pioneer look to them, but the place where Dunn was shot, called Nevin's, no longer exists.

Killing time at the Hagerman Lake lumber camp.

MURDERING MARY

THE YEAR: 1887 – 1903
THE CRIME: MURDER
THE MOTIVE: SHE LIKED FUNERALS

FEMALE SERIAL KILLERS ARE RARE.

And if it happens, the victims are usually people known to the killer, people whom they've cared for — like spouses, and children in particular. In this way, Mary McKnight, an unusually prolific serial killer, was run-of-the-mill. Her trail of 12 related corpses — some put the number at 18 — criss-crossed the Lower Peninsula.

Early death was common then. Childbirth, infection, and disease were all lethal. Almost no one lived beyond the age of 50. So no one noticed the ghoulish baggage Mary dragged around. They felt sorry for her.

Her undoing came at the hands of a Kalkaska County prosecutor and coroner. They smelled foul play when young John Murphy, his bride Gertrude, and their infant daughter, Ruth, died excruciating, convulsive deaths within days of each other.

The two men undertook the unpleasant job of digging up the coffins — there were only two, as the mother had been buried with her arms around her daughter. When the contents of the Murphy stomachs were sent to a lab downstate, technicians easily distinguished a common rat poison as the killer.

Actually, Mary was the killer. She'd killed her own brother, John Murphy and his family. Turns out she'd also killed her own husband awhile back. And her sister. And a niece, and another niece, and a second husband, and a daughter and another daughter….

Strychnine causes some of the most violent reactions of known toxins. First, there's the cold sweat, a metallic taste in the mouth, flashing lights. The spasms will begin in the neck, then spread. Its victims double up in pain until the continuous convulsions freeze their spines into a broken arch. Their last fevered dreams are often ones of intense fear and paranoia. Death comes within two or three hours, of asphyxia.

The Murphy case finally put into question poor Mary McKnight's long history of lost loved ones. It turned out that she'd been killing the people she lived with or visited for fifteen years. A surviving sister provided a possible motive.

"Mary just likes funerals," she said.

Granted, socializing and dress-up occasions were few and far between in the rural areas she inhabited. A funeral could be a break in the lonely, isolated land of long winters littered with pine stumps. She liked to dress up, and her prized piece of clothing was the black dress she'd pull out of the closet at funeral time.

Still, you can't ignore the money motive. That $4,000 total she collected in insurance for her two husbands was the equivalent of about $115,000 now. Not to mention that she tried to claim insurance money after the death of John Murphy.

Mary was arrested in Walton Junction, a long-gone lumberjack saloon-and-brothel town. She was getting on a train to Traverse City.

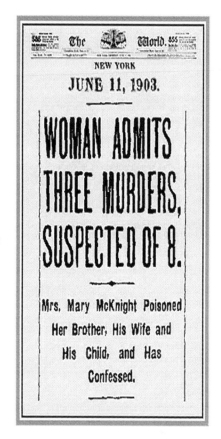

NEW YORK

JUNE 11, 1903.

WOMAN ADMITS THREE MURDERS, SUSPECTED OF 8.

Mrs. Mary McKnight Poisoned Her Brother, His Wife and His Child, and Has Confessed.

A painting from 1809 that shows the spasm effects of strychnine poisoning.

Something to Quiet Them

Mary McKnight voluntarily confessed to the murders of her brother and his family. The confession was printed in the Semi-Weekly Cedar Falls Gazette on June 26, 1903:

"The baby woke up and cried while its mother was gone, and I mixed up a little strychnine in a glass with some water and gave a spoonful to the baby. I didn't mean to harm the little thing at all. I confessed all to the Lord this afternoon, and I feel that he has forgiven me.

"When Gertrude came home and found the baby dead, she got awfully nervous. She came to me and said: 'Mary, can't you give me something to quiet me; something that you take yourself?' I said that I would, and I really didn't think that it would hurt her if I gave her one of the capsules. She had spasms right after that, and I suppose that It was the strychnine that killed her. I really didn't mean to hurt her.

"Then John seemed to feel so badly about it, so broken up, that I often thought after Gertie died that it would be better if he were to go, too. John was feeling bad one night a couple of weeks after Gertrude died. He came to me and wanted something to quiet him. I had two or three of the capsules on my dresser, and I told him to go and get one of them.

"I didn't mean to hurt him, but I thought that it would soothe him, and then I thought that it would be for the best if he were to go, anyway. He helped himself, I don't know whether he took one or two. Then he went to bed, and by and by he called me. Mother came, too, and he began to have those same spasms. I suppose that the strychnine was working."

Mary was paroled from the Detroit House of Corrections after 18 years.

FOLLOW THE STRYCHNINE 12

If you want to follow Mary McKnight's poison path, begin in Alpena.

Husband J.D. Ambrose had his sign-painting shop on Chisholm Street. Chisholm is one of the central roads for businesses. It's now part of **M-23**, the town's entrance from the northwest.

You could take a side trip down to Saginaw, via **M-23**, which hugs the Lake Huron shoreline. It goes through sunrise-side towns of Oscoda and Tawas City, with lighthouses, and stops for picnicking and shoreline exploration.

Alpena to Grayling is a straight shot over to Gaylord on **M-32** and down **I-75**, or a jagged, scenic angling down county roads to the southwest, through Lewiston and other towns. Then from Grayling, go west to Kalkaska and down **U.S. 31** to Fife Lake.

Clark Cemetery at **Coster** and **Shippy** roads east of Fife Lake is a shaded, peaceful place for a final rest. But if you wander through and find the graves of John and Gertrude Murphy next to each other, know that poor little Ruth Murphy is there buried nestled in her mother's arms. Sadly, she's not listed on the marker.

Mary's incarceration was at Detroit House of Corrections (DeHoCo), which was between Northville and Plymouth and close to where Jack Keyes' body was found (see page 92).

THE WITCH OF DELRAY

THE YEAR: 1925 – 1931
THE CRIME: MURDER
THE MOTIVE: LUCRE

ROSE VERES KNEW HOW TO MAKE OLD WORLD SUPERSTITIONS WORK FOR HER.

Veres owned a boarding house in a Westside Detroit enclave of Hungarian immigrants neighboring a steel mill. She took a lot of men into her home, many whom were down on their luck. In fact, bad luck may have been a calling card of hers.

Rumors that she was bewitched swirled around the ethnic neighborhood. She encouraged the whispering and declared herself a shape-shifter. Oh, the power of persuasion. It wasn't long before someone claimed to have seen her morph into animals in the moonlight. But the Evil Eye was her contrivance of choice: a menacing look almost guaranteed death. As one neighbor said, "She boasts that she cannot stay in jail, that she knows the magic to get out. We are afraid to catch her eye. She can make our children sick and our husbands lose their jobs. She knows all kinds of magic."

This dark mystique gave her a wide berth in Delray. Any questions about the black magic landlord and folks became hushed and evasive, even as the deaths piled up.

In the mid-20s, and after two of her tenants died of severe alcohol poisoning, the cops came calling. No one talked. Superstition minus evidence does not a conviction make. Police let her go.

Shortly thereafter, in another twofer, Rose's second husband, Gabor Veres, and another man died of carbon monoxide poisoning. They were working on a car in a garage while the vehicle idled. Someone quietly closed the door and they were asphyxiated. Mum was once again the word.

But by 1931, things were changing in the neighborhood. Black families from the South were starting to move to Delray. They either hadn't heard of or didn't put much stock in the reports of Rose Veres's supernatural powers.

While a Little Girl Watched the Old Gray Witch of Medina Street—

—*The Hungarian Widow's Twelfth Boarder Tumbled to His Death, But Marie of the Mud Pies Saw All, and Told!*

From the Ogden Standard Examiner, April 3, 1932.

So when 68-year-old tenant Steve Mak fell from a third-story window to his death, several of the new neighbors, including children, gave the police detectives an earful. Mak was supposed to have fallen off a ladder — witnesses said he was pushed out a window.

Examinations of the body found injuries that weren't like your usual fall-off-the-ladder type. Although someone leaned a ladder against the house before Mak's fall, the evidence seemed to support the neighbors' skepticism.

Mak's death was the thread that unraveled Rose's murderous web. Further investigation found that a total of 12 men died under mysterious circumstances while staying in her house. She even hosted some of the men's funerals.

Turns out, Rose had taken out life insurance policies on her tenants, so a funeral was the least she could do. The boarders may have been poor in life, but they paid off in death.

She claimed it was commonplace in Hungary to take out policies on one's tenants — in Delray it raised eyebrows.

Still, police charged her only with Mak's murder. She was sentenced to life in prison, though she was acquitted in a re-trial in 1945.

MURDER MAP

Rose Veres's boarding house was on **Medina Street**, in an area known as Delray. Delray was once a separate town bordering Detroit, but was annexed into the city in the early 20th century.

Delray's Hungarian population came there for jobs in the steel mills and lived in the same neighborhood where they worked. While the 1930 Census showed 23,000 people living in that section of the city, it's about one-tenth of that now. That's not necessarily a bad thing, though, since decades of heavy industry have polluted the air and rendered it a less-than-desirable place to live.

Delray fronts the Detroit River and is across the River Rouge from the industrial site Zug Island and the city of River Rouge.

On the other side of Delray is Historic Fort Wayne, built in 1843 to guard against the British. The fort frequently hosts historic reenactments and an occasional ghost tour.

BAD BISCUITS

THE YEAR: 1905
THE CRIME: MURDER
THE MOTIVE: DEMOTION

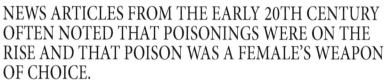

NEWS ARTICLES FROM THE EARLY 20TH CENTURY OFTEN NOTED THAT POISONINGS WERE ON THE RISE AND THAT POISON WAS A FEMALE'S WEAPON OF CHOICE.

It made sense, in light of the rigid gender roles of the time. Women were the home-keepers and did the cooking in most families. Arsenic, like strychnine, was a popular household rat killer. Its ingestion, however, leads to a most indelicate demise, hardly even worthy of a rat. Only after hours of diarrhea, vomiting and abdominal pain does Death apply its cool, white hand.

Rose Barron is widely believed to have slipped the caustic element into biscuits fed to 10 wealthy families who called the stylish Alhambra Apartments home. Maybe she'd read about poison in the newspaper, or maybe she'd seen a rat die. In any case, the police believed she was driven to murder after her employers demoted her from cook to scrubwoman. Kind of makes you wonder, though: if Rose Barron did poison the biscuits, did she think it through? Given the symptoms of an arsenic death, the poisonings wouldn't have made the duties of a scrubwoman any more pleasant?

The dosage was not lethal for all of those who ate the biscuits. Only two people died, while many others got sick. Rose Barron ultimately walked away from the charges because the medical examiners of the day weren't able to find the poison in the victims' bodies.

MURDER MAP

Alhambra Apartments were at **Temple** and **Park**, but you'd have to squint pretty hard to see that the surrounding area was once the site of upper class apartments.

The building itself is another story. It is still standing tall and holding its antique charm, at least on the outside, with turrets and bay windows. There had been talk that it may come down for the new Red Wings hockey arena going up nearby, though there is a renewed interest in historic buildings of that neighborhood.

What's left of The Alhambra Apartments is about a block and a half from the Masonic Temple, itself a Detroit gem. Built in 1926, it claims to be the world's largest Masonic temple. It still houses several organizations related to the Masons, and has been well-known as a premier concert venue in recent decades.

The stage is renowned for its fine acoustics and has played host to Duke Ellington, Bob Dylan, Ray Charles, Iggy Pop and David Bowie together, plus dozens of other music legends.

Detroit rocker Jack White, formerly of the White Stripes, has also played there. In 2013, he paid $142,000 in back taxes to save it from foreclosure. The owners have renamed one of the stages in the complex the Jack White Theater.

The Alhambra Apartments
in good times.

A Tale of Two Poisons

Arsenic is a common element found on the earth and in the atmosphere. It is essential — in trace amounts — for the health of goats, chickens, hamsters and, yes, humans. Human contact with arsenic goes back at least 5000 years. A lot of it was found in the "Iceman" uncovered in the Italian Alps in 1991, probably absorbed while he worked with metals. The Persians used it for gilding and the Chinese as a pesticide. Italy and France used it for the removal of popes they didn't like, and in WWI, Americans used it as a chemical weapon, lewisite. It caused terrible blisters on the skin and in the lungs if inhaled.

It's not surprising that the element was a popular murder weapon in the U.S. and the U.K. in the 1900s. It was cheap and easy to get. As a household rat poison, it wouldn't have turned any heads showing up in a kitchen cabinet. A small amount is fatal and easily hidden in food, giving off little flavor.

What's more, the symptoms — including vomiting and diarrhea — could be confused for several illnesses, including cholera, the flu or dysentery. In light of the hundreds of poisoning cases that were found out, there were probably a lot more that never aroused suspicion.

Laws made arsenic harder to get in the 20th century, and forensic science has become increasingly equipped to detect such things.

A strychnine death, on the other hand, is sudden and violent. The convulsing and tensing of muscles, the gasping for air and the death within as little as two hours, was unlikely to be confused with a common illness. Still, it has also been used as a murder weapon throughout history. Macedonian king Alexander the Great may have been killed by strychnine slipped into his wine in 323 B.C.

CONTAGIOUS GREED

THE YEAR: 1916
THE CRIME: MURDER
THE MOTIVE: TOO SMALL AN ALLOWANCE

ARTHUR WAITE WAS SOMETHING OF A RENAISSANCE MAN.

The son of a grocer, he got himself into the University of Michigan to study dentistry, then did his oral surgery residency in record time in Scotland. He traveled the world, spoke several languages and played quality amateur tennis. He could sing, dance, and best of all, he was tall and handsome. He was so accomplished that Clara Peck of Grand Rapids couldn't believe her good luck when he came a-courting.

Clara was the daughter of John Peck, a Grand Rapids native who'd amassed a fortune by investing his drug store profits in real estate, timber, furniture and banking. Peck had so much money that after his daughter's wedding to Waite, he bought and furnished an apartment for them at the ritzy Colosseum on Riverside in New York City.

Then the troubles began, and the troubles were money. These were the days of bride dowries — money paid by the father to help support the daughter — and Peck had promised a doozy — $50,000, over a million in today's market. Waite wanted the whole caboodle in one big lump sum. Peck wasn't having it. In fact, he was doling it out at a safe $300 a month. (Actually, that would be worth about $7,000 these days, so they weren't exactly starving.)

The Waites were married in the fall, and just after Christmas, they invited Mother Peck to visit them in New York. Only hours after she arrived, she was complaining of stomach pains. She was dead before the end of the year. When Father Peck developed the same symptoms in March — also during a visit to New York — and died shortly thereafter, someone smelled a rat.

The rat, of course, was Waite. And while he could have bought some rat poison to score his wife's fortune, living microscopic organisms were more the style of an accomplished Renaissance man. He tried several germs — flu, diphtheria, typhoid, anthrax — and dosed everything the Peck parents ingested for breakfast, lunch and dinner. The results were spectacular with Mrs. Peck, but the mister must have had an iron immune system. Waite got impatient and resorted to arsenic, chloroform and, eventually, smothering — with a pillow. He knew his treachery would show up in an autopsy and begged the relatives back in Grand Rapids to proceed directly to cremation.

A week later, Waite was behind bars. Turns out he was a total fake. He could certainly sing and dance, but he was no surgeon. At his trial, he claimed insanity. It didn't work. Waite was sent to Sing Sing Prison in New York, where he was executed by 2,000 volts. He was thirty years old.

Drug stores in 1916 looked more like a New Age dispensary crossed with an opium den than a Walgreens of today. Pharmacists worked primarily with crude drugs, in other words, powders, extracts and distillations of naturally sourced materials, usually herbs. Prescriptions were based on the accumulated knowledge of human experimentation going back to prehistoric times. A typical pharmacy would stock:

Bismuth (an intestinal deodorant)

Autumn crocus (for gout)

Gambir (premature ejaculation)

Scapula (a hypnotic and analgesic)

Silver nitrate (warts)

Aloe

Vanilla

Whiskey

Suet

Heroin

Laudanum

Opium

Cocaine

Quinine

And the extracts of everything from bitter orange peel to digitalis, cannabis and rhubarb.

By the way, Oxycodone was developed in Germany in 1916 as an attempt to improve on the existing painkiller trinity of morphine, heroin and codeine. Germany had introduced heroin in the 1870s as a — get this — cure for morphine addiction.

Image shows an Ely Lilly crude drug specimen case for pharmacy students. These samplers were standard issue for pharmacy students until the 1950s.

DEATH BY APPOINTMENT

THE YEAR: 1990s
THE CRIME: MURDER?
THE MOTIVE: RIGHT TO DIE

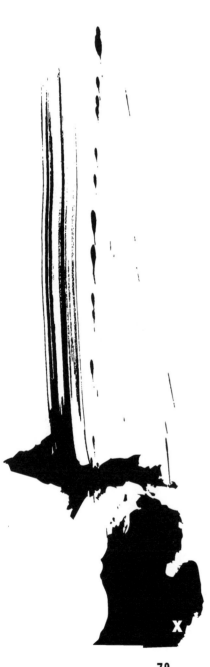

WHETHER OR NOT YOU CONSIDER DR. JACK KEVORKIAN A MURDERER LIKELY DEPENDS ON YOUR OPINIONS OF ASSISTED SUICIDE.

Kevorkian, a Royal Oak physician, claimed to have helped 130 or so people with terminal illnesses end their lives in the 1990s. He served eight years in prison for second-degree murder.

When the wiry, cardigan-wearing Kevorkian burst onto the scene and the national consciousness, he had just hooked a woman with Alzheimer's to his "suicide machine." The device — which he built himself on his kitchen table and called the Mercitron — released carbon monoxide into a face mask that slowly filled the patient's lungs, shutting down her body. It also dispensed calming and pain-killing drugs to make for a — hopefully — comfortable ending. The patient turned the knob that set the final steps in motion, and Kevorkian attended as the patient drifted off. He monitored vitals to make sure she was dead, then calmly called the police to report the passing.

That was pretty much how it went each time, frequently resulting in his arrest and release. As word got out, others contacted him to help them exit their lives of pain and deterioration on their own terms. His now famously colorful lawyer, Geoffrey Fieger, did the talking to the cameras.

Quickly, Kevorkian became an international symbol of both mercy and murder. Instant celebrity and punchline, he was the face of a brand new movement to allow people to choose the precise times and causes of their deaths — as long as they were dying already. Some who supported his cause wished that he were more discrete. Pictures of the doctor smiling next to his grim device didn't help. Among colleagues, he had a reputation for obsession with the morbid. The media celebrated when they caught him in one of his favorite leisure activities — painting macabre scenes of severed heads and skulls on canvasses in his austere apartment.

Still, like it or not, he brought the issue into the public eye. People with cancer, Lou Gehrig's disease and AIDS were reaching out to him as the only dignified option to end their suffering.

He performed his Michigan services around the Detroit area, and as far away as Leelanau County. Patients died in their homes or cottages, others in his Volkswagen bus.

As Michigan and other states grappled with laws on an issue that was non-existent a few years earlier, he was brought to trial four times in Michigan: he got three acquittals and one mistrial.

Then, in 1999, he circulated a video of an assisted suicide. Some thought he was taunting the police and he was arrested again. This time he was tried and convicted of second-degree murder. Kevorkian served eight years in prison and died in 2011 at the age of 83 at William Beaumont Hospital in Royal Oak. He had suffered from liver cancer, pneumonia and chronic kidney problems.

Debate continues on the assisted suicide issue, as well as whether all of Kevorkian's patients were actually terminal.

MURDER MAP

Kevorkian is buried at White Chapel Memorial Cemetery in Troy. The University of Michigan, his alma mater, has added his archived records to its Bentley Historical Library in Ann Arbor.

Detail from "Coma," an original oil painting by Jack Kevorkian.

73

"Apotheosis" by Vasily Vereshchagin

AMERICA'S BLOODIEST BATTLEFIELD

THE YEAR: 1812
THE CRIME: MURDER
THE MOTIVE: WAR

IT'S CALLED THE BATTLE OF FRENCHTOWN OR THE RIVER RAISIN MASSACRE.

Both are part of what is commonly called The War of 1812.

It all started in Detroit, where in the summer of 1812, the British defeated the Americans at Fort Detroit. Anxious to head off an all-out British take-over of Michigan Territory, the Americans scrambled to assemble a new force capable of reclaiming the outpost that winter. The idea was to gather outside Frenchtown (present day Monroe, 35 miles south), retake the town, then move forward to a showdown in Detroit.

The American army was split into two columns, one of which consisted of mostly raw recruits from Kentucky. This column was ordered to keep back from the main fighting, but Second-in-Command James Winchester disobeyed the order, sending a small detachment to sneak in along the frozen Lake Erie shore to the River Raisin. It worked and they reclaimed Frenchtown. Too bad the troops then rested on their laurels. Supplies were left behind at the Maumee River and the palisades unrepaired while troops camped willy-nilly outside the fort's walls.

Four days later, their enemies returned, attacking the Americans in their sleep. They killed 397 U.S. soldiers outright and took another 547 as prisoners. It was the greatest victory for Tecumseh's American Indian confederation, not to mention the British. For the United States, it was the war's greatest defeat.

And it wasn't over. The next day, those too seriously wounded in the field were killed and the rest marched to Fort Malden in Ontario. Remember, this is January, and soldiers who couldn't keep up were killed.

The large loss helped inspire the American side for the rest of the war, as "Remember the Raisin" became a rallying cry. Nine counties in Kentucky are named for fallen River Raisin officers.

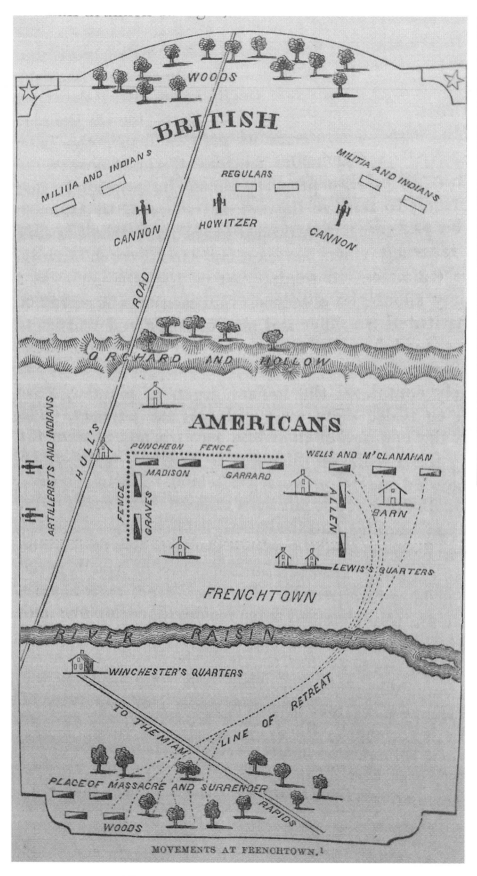

WOODS

BRITISH

MILITIA AND INDIANS

REGULARS

MILITIA AND INDIANS

CANNON

HOWITZER

CANNON

ROAD

ORCHARD AND HOLLOW

ARTILLERISTS AND INDIANS

HULL'S

AMERICANS

PUNCHEON FENCE

WELLS AND M'CLANAHAN

FENCE

MADISON

GARRARD

ALLEN

BARN

GRAVES

LEWIS'S QUARTERS

FRENCHTOWN

RIVER RAISIN

WINCHESTER'S QUARTERS

TO THE MIAMI

LINE OF RETREAT

RAPIDS

PLACE OF MASSACRE AND SURRENDER

WOODS

MOVEMENTS AT FRENCHTOWN, 1

The core area of the battle is bounded by **North Dixie Highway**, the River Raisin, **Detroit Avenue**, and Mason Run Creek.

In 2010, the battle site was upgraded by Congress to the River Raisin National Battlefield Park, part of the National Park Service. There are only four other National Battlefield sites in the United States, and River Raisin is the only battle site that commemorates the War of 1812.

The remains of Crow Indians killed and scalped by Sioux around 1874.

Is War Murder?

To some, killing is killing. One human being taking another's life knowingly equals murder. To others there is a philosophical question when it comes to war. For a soldier, it's in the job description.

There are heroic actions in war, to be sure; like staying with a wounded buddy without regard for one's own safety. Or, when Gen. George Custer, on the spur of the moment, rode his horse headlong into danger, leading the Michigan Cavalry to turn back Rebel riders in the Battle of Gettysburg.

But there are also acts that most would consider wrong, like the killing of unarmed civilians. Or, again, when Gen. George Custer, on the spur of the moment, rode his horse headlong into a peaceful camp of Cheyenne Indians, leading the slaughter of the wrong people. And of course, there are the everyday actions of soldiers in battle — the fog of war can be very gray. So is war murder?

Here's a bit of that debate in quotes:

It is my conviction that killing under the cloak of war is nothing but an act of murder.
—Physicist Albert Einstein, who helped design history's most deadly weapon

The object of war is not to die for your country but to make the other bastard die for his.
—General George S. Patton, aka "Old Blood and Guts," who led the U.S. Third Army in France and Germany following the invasion of Normandy

Ef you take a sword an' dror it / An go stick a feller thru, / Guv'ment aint to answer to it, / God'll send the bill to you.
—19th century satirist James Russell Lowell

The true soldier fights not because he hates what is in front of him, but because he loves what is behind him. —English author and philosopher, G.K. Chesterton

SHOOT FIRST, THINK LATER

THE YEAR: 1868
THE CRIME: MURDER
THE MOTIVE: GLORY

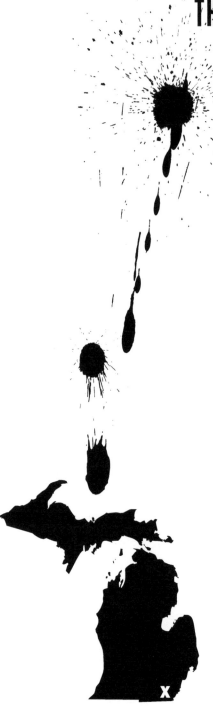

GENERAL GEORGE ARMSTRONG CUSTER, A MICHIGANDER REARED IN MONROE, MADE HIS FAMOUS LAST STAND AT THE BATTLE OF LITTLE BIGHORN IN SOUTHERN MONTANA.

More than Custer's last stand, it was the last major victory for the American Indians, who had been all but wiped out as Europeans settled throughout North America.

Custer was born in eastern Ohio, the son of a blacksmith, but he grew up in Monroe in the home of his half-sister. He attended West Point, where he received constant demerits for pulling pranks on his classmates, was arrested for failing to stop a fight and graduated last in his class.

Yet he worked his way up to captain in the Union Army during the Civil War, often fighting gallantly and aggressively, most notably at the Battle of Gettysburg. There, as the Union Army's left flank was threatened by Confederate cavalry and had begun to retreat, Custer broke through to the front of the 1st Michigan Cavalry, dressed in his black velvet uniform, saber poised above his head. He galloped into the fray, yelling "Come on, you Wolverines!" and helped flip the Confederate momentum.

But the flamboyant military man with his long, blond ringlets, flashy uniforms, bushy mustache and soul patch is better known for what he did after the Civil War. It was in the government's campaign to rid the Great Plains of the people who had occupied it for millennia that Custer truly made his name.

In 1868, he led the U.S. forces to what they considered their first victory in the Indian wars at Washita River in Oklahoma. If he'd done his homework, he could have easily found out the Cheyenne encampment was a peaceful community on federal reservation land that had been promised safety by a nearby fort commander. Cocky and off-the-cuff, Custer didn't ask, merely assumed this was the band that had led raids on white settlers. He had his men surround the camp and charge in from all sides at dawn. They slaughtered 103 men, women and children. Custer also killed their ponies, all 875 of them.

Because of Washita River and other similar incidents, what happened later at Little Big Horn was viewed with scorn within days after it happened.

It began in June, 1876, when Sitting Bull, a Lakota holy man, led a confederation of Cheyenne and Lakota — plus others who'd managed to slip their reservation boundaries — to a Sun Dance, the holiest of days for the Plains Tribes. During the ceremony, Sitting Bull had a vision in which he saw "soldiers falling into his camp like grasshoppers from the sky."

At the same time, government forces under Custer's command were organizing a major campaign to force the plains tribes securely onto reservations. Custer, arrogant as usual, assured the troops that the Seventh Cavalry "could handle anything." He grossly underestimated the size of the opposing force and 268 U.S. soldiers, or more than one third of the 7th Cavalry, including the general, two of his brothers and other relatives, were wiped out. The Lakota call the rout the Battle of Greasy Grass.

News of the loss reached the public during the Fourth of July Centennial celebrations, and President Ulysses S. Grant was quoted in the *New York Herald*, saying: "I regard Custer's Massacre as a sacrifice of troops, brought on by Custer himself, that was wholly unnecessary — wholly unnecessary."

MURDER MAP

Monroe, Michigan's largest city on Lake Erie, has a historical museum known for its Custer exhibits on the site where the general and his wife once lived. A statue of him on horseback here was dedicated in 1910 by President William Howard Taft and Custer's widow.

The Monroe County Historical Museum & George A. Custer Exhibit is at **126 South Monroe Street**.

Death of Custer scene from Pawnee Bill's 1905 Wild West Show. Sitting Bull is shown stabbing Custer.

Goats Get Their Due

Graduating last in your class at the United States Military Academy at West Point, like George Armstrong Custer did in 1861, is not as embarrassing as it might seem.

Since 1886, fellow graduates have "honored" the cadet who squeaks through by the narrowest margin as the class Goat. Everyone kicks in a buck for the near failure, and they give the Goat the loudest applause of the commencement.

Custer wasn't the only Goat who achieved fame in the Battle of Gettysburg. Major General George Pickett of the Confederate Army was also a last-place West Pointer. Pickett is best known for the courageous, but utterly disastrous, Pickett's Charge in the pivotal Civil War battle.

Tecumseh

It's unclear why the town of Tecumseh — halfway between Monroe and Jackson — took its name from the Shawnee chief. Perhaps he gave the land to its original settlers, as he did in Frenchtown.

Or maybe a founder just "took a fancy" to the man, like the father of William Tecumseh Sherman, General of the Union Army and Confederate scourge.

Canadians honor Tecumseh as a hero and outstanding speaker: "Live your life so that the fear of death can never enter your heart...Love your life, perfect your life, beautify all things in your life. Seek to make your life long and in the service of your people..."

BLOOD BATH

THE YEAR: 1927
THE CRIME: MURDER
THE MOTIVE: TAXES

THE WORST MASS MURDER OF SCHOOL CHILDREN IN U.S. HISTORY WAS COMMITTED BY AN ANTI-TAX SCHOOL BOARD MEMBER IN DANGER OF LOSING HIS FARM.

Sound like recent history? Guess again. This was May, 1927 — two days before Charles Lindbergh set off on his historic trans-Atlantic flight.

The killer was Andrew Kehoe, born in Tecumseh, a graduate of Michigan State, a farmer and a bit of a dandy. He used to drive a tractor in an immaculate vested suit and freshly shined shoes. His tractors were state-of-the-art for the day, shiny like they'd just come from a showroom.

That did make other farmers lift their sweated caps and scratch their heads. But he made friends, in part by sharing his explosives expertise whenever someone needed a tree stump removed. His Fourth of July celebrations made people jump for miles around.

But the farmers were right. There was something different about Kehoe. For one thing, he was mean as dirt and was once observed beating a horse to death. When he was a teenager, the kitchen stove exploded, spraying his step-mother with fuel oil that then caught on fire. He unhelpfully threw water on her. And there was his wife, fading away slowly and expensively by tuberculosis. About the time he stopped paying his mortgage, he also lost his treasurer position on the school board. Voters were tired of his relentless fight against taxes of all kinds — particularly the millage proposal to build a new school. Slow-burning resentment and Kehoe's quiet, murderous way were about to blow up.

But first, the school got built. A great, big, stately pile with two large wings. Kehoe had done the electrical wiring and was the unofficial handyman, so it didn't seem weird when, over a period of several months, he toiled away at the basement. Little did they know that he was packing dynamite and the explosive pyrotol into the nooks and crannies of both the north and south wings. Kehoe spaced them out methodically and wired them to a school clock.

He finished mid-May. The work done, he went home, killed his wife, moved her to a barn and blew up the farm. At precisely 8:45 a.m. on the morning of May 18, as some classes had story time and others did morning exercises, the school's north wing exploded. The blast killed 38 children and 6 adults, and blew out windows in nearby homes.

As rescuers desperately sifted through bricks and boards and rubble, searching for survivors, Kehoe drove up. He climbed out of his vehicle, picked a fight with the school superintendent, then fired his rifle into his truck, setting off the dynamite and shrapnel packed inside. The superintendent, another man, an 8-year-old boy who had survived the first blast and Kehoe himself all died, bringing the final, murderous toll to 45 dead and 58 injured.

When authorities went out to the Kehoe farm after the bombing, they found a wooden sign wired to a fence with the phrase, "Criminals are made, not born" stenciled on it. Kehoe's last words.

MURDER MAP

Bath is a few miles northeast of Lansing. On its outskirts are lakefront homes and cottages, and relatively recent subdivisions and condos.

There's a lonely park where the school stood. That school building, once the pride of the town and its focal point, is gone. There are still some old homes from the era of the bombing and a small row of businesses. The triangular memorial park is 2.5 miles north of I-69, off the **Webster Road** exit. It's on the west side of Webster, between **Clark** and **Sleight** roads.

A cupola stands as a sad reminder. This is not the one that stood atop the school when Kehoe decided to seek revenge by killing school children. It's a reproduction put in place after Bath Consolidated was rebuilt onto the remains of the old building.

The serene and understated memorial site also has a state historical marker and a plaque listing the victims.

Across the road is Bath Middle School, which contains a museum devoted to the bombing. The exhibit includes the flag flown there that horrible day and bricks from the building. The museum is open by appointment when the school is in session.

Andrew Philip Kehoe is buried in an unmarked grave in St. Johns.

SECOND ONLY TO BIN LADEN

THE YEAR: 1995
THE CRIME: MURDER
THE MOTIVE: GOVERNMENT

TERRY NICHOLS AND TIMOTHY MCVEIGH
MASTERMINDED A PLOT TO KILL MORE U.S.
CITIZENS AT ONE TIME THAN ANY OTHER
DOMESTIC TERRORISTS IN HISTORY.

When you include foreign terrorists, they're second only to
Osama bin Laden.

The plot was hatched at the farm of Terry's brother, James
Nichols, in Sanilac County in the middle of the Thumb. They
did it in the name of patriotism.

Nichols and McVeigh met in the Army and bonded over
extreme right-wing politics. After his service, Nichols
returned to the farm and renounced his American citizenship,
claiming the government had no authority over him. McVeigh
immersed himself in one conspiracy theory after another.
But the two kept in touch and happened to be watching the
news together at James Nichols' house when the disastrous
government siege in Waco, Texas, came to a head. After a 51-
day standoff between federal agents and a religious sect known
as the Branch Davidians — suspected of weapons violations
— 76 members of the group, including children, died as the
compound burned to the ground.

Many Americans were angry. Anti-government sentiments
seethed, and private militia groups sprang up in rural
communities in Michigan and elsewhere. Nichols and
McVeigh went beyond angry. They planned to get even. Two
years later, on the anniversary of the Waco debacle, their plan
would detonate.

Begin the countdown: With 11 days to go, McVeigh tells
a stripper in a Tulsa, Arizona, club, "On April 19th, you'll
remember me for the rest of my life."

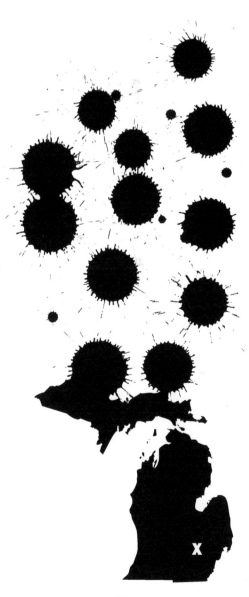

With three days to go, McVeigh and Nichols drive to Oklahoma City in separate vehicles so McVeigh can leave his there as a getaway car.

With one day to go, they meet at a storage unit and load a rented Ryder moving truck with 3.5 tons of fertilizer, nitromethane and diesel fuel.

April 19, 1995. Timothy McVeigh put on a t-shirt with a picture of Abe Lincoln and a quote from his assassin, John Wilkes Booth: "Sic Semper Tyrannis," Latin for "Thus always to tyrants." He climbed in the rental truck and drove to the Alfred P. Murrah Federal Building, the local location of the Bureau of Alcohol, Tobacco, Firearms and Explosives, the agency responsible for the Waco disaster. However, the building also housed several other agencies and an employee day care center. The bomb was set up so that the chemical fertilizer reacted with fuel oil. McVeigh lit a timed fuse, locked the doors, and hurried to his getaway car.

At 9:02 a.m., as many of the office workers/"tyrants" were likely pouring coffee or booting up their computers, the truck exploded and collapsed the front half of the building. The blast killed 168 people — including 19 children and a few people in nearby buildings or parking lots. It seriously damaged more than 300 nearby buildings.

About an hour later, police pulled McVeigh over for driving without license plates while heading north on I-35 toward Wichita, Kansas. They found a gun in the car and arrested him. McVeigh gave his home address as Decker, Michigan.

Nichols made it home to his farm, possibly thinking he'd get away with it if he laid low for a while. However, when his and McVeigh's handiwork dominated the news day after day, he started feeling the pinch. As the police sifted through evidence and questioned McVeigh, clues started pointing toward that farm in the Thumb. On April 21, he turned himself in after hearing he was a suspect.

McVeigh, for his hands-on part in the worst domestic terrorist act ever, was executed by lethal injection in 2001.

Nichols was sentenced to life in prison without parole and is living out his days at a federal prison near Florence, Colorado. He shares a cell block with "Unabomber" Ted Kaczynski and one of the terrorists involved in the 1993 World Trade Center bombing.

MURDER MAP

The farm where Nichols and McVeigh planned their massacre of federal workers was near Decker, Michigan, at **3596 North Van Dyke Road** in the middle of flat farm country.

In Oklahoma City, there's a memorial now at the site of the Alfred P. Murrah Building. It consists of rows of empty chairs to symbolize the victims.

OPEN CARRY

THE YEAR: 1998
THE CRIME: MURDER
THE MOTIVE: PARANOIA

NEIGHBORS AMONG THE STATELY LUMBER-BARON HOMES NEAR DOWNTOWN TRAVERSE CITY KNEW JOHN CLARK AS A QUIET BUT INTENSE AND PARANOID GUY.

A tall thin man with white hair and beard, he could almost be a character acted by Christopher Lloyd — Marty McFly's scientist chum in "Back to the Future."

They didn't really think he was dangerous, though people didn't go out of their way to talk to him. If they did, he was likely to launch into obsessive rantings about the mafia controlling the local government and the cops. Or he'd boast about the impressive arsenal of guns he had in his basement. He'd also taken to wearing a sidearm while doing yard work.

May was a great time to be doing yard work. Traverse Citians often spend warm spring afternoons enjoying the relative quiet before Memorial Day marks the arrival of tourist season and the town transforms into a crowded beach resort.

Spring was in bloom on just such an afternoon when a nervous neighbor called the police to say Clark was armed and seemed upset. Sergeant Dennis Finch, a 30-year veteran of the Traverse City Police Department — which had never lost an officer to violence — came to see if he could calm Clark down and get him to put his gun away.

As they talked, Clark retreated to the grandly pillared porch of the home in which he and his mother lived. Other officers arrived to stand by, as the tension between Finch and Clark wasn't easing up.

Then, when Clark turned to go inside, Finch hopped on the porch with his gun drawn. Clark heard his move and quickly turned around, his semi-automatic blazing.

Sgt. Finch receives medical attention after being shot.

Record-Eagle, May 13, 1998

Two shots to the mid-section and Finch fell on the edge of the porch, bleeding badly. Other shots were fired after the first shot rang out. Two officers, one who had been sneaking under the porch, rushed over and dragged Finch toward an ambulance.

More reinforcements came quickly and Clark retreated inside, warning police he was heavily armed. For several tense hours, officers tried to talk him out as neighbors laid low, peering out the safest window they could find. Finally, after midnight, Clark gave up and laid down on the floor inside his house. The police rushed in, several training their rifles on him while another slapped the cuffs on him.

Finch died before morning.

During the trial, Clark's defense claimed that Finch was hit by friendly fire — that police opened fire after the initial shots and may have actually fired the bullets that killed the sergeant. That argument was unsuccessful, and Clark was sentenced to life in prison.

MURDER MAP

The Victorian home where shots rang out from the porch is at the corner of **Wellington** and **Washington** streets, a few blocks southeast of downtown Traverse City. It's now a bed & breakfast.

A few blocks further south at **851 Woodmere Avenue** is the Sgt. Dennis W. Finch Law Enforcement Center, built after his murder and named in his honor.

HE CAN'T QUIT HER

THE YEAR: 1985
THE CRIME: MURDER
THE MOTIVE: THE END OF THE GRAVY TRAIN

IT WAS PSYCHOLOGIST DR. ALAN CANTY, JR.'S FIFTIETH BIRTHDAY AND HIS WIFE WAS OUT OF TOWN.

What better excuse to take a spin during his lunch hour down to the then-infamous Cass Corridor to ogle the streetwalkers?

There stood eighteen-year-old Dawn Spens. She was attractive and smart — a former A-student from Harper Woods. She was also a heroin addict. Barely old enough to vote, she did a decent business for a streetwalker. Against a backdrop of mostly older women who'd had a much longer relationship with the needle, she looked fresh. Best of all, she could afford, because of her youth, to solicite in broad daylight instead of waiting for the cover of night.

The balding, bespectacled Dr. Canty invited Dawn into his warm car on that November day in 1983. He chatted with her for a bit, then asked her for a phone number. She gave it to him, even though her boyfriend and pimp, John "Lucky" Fry, wouldn't like it. She also figured he wouldn't call. She was wrong. Dr. Canty called later that afternoon, picked her up, and drove to the Temple Hotel. The $100 bill he left on the bed was about as lucky as Lucky Fry could have wished for.

Even better for Lucky, this would become a regular thing.

Almost two years went by, and the doctor's relationship with Dawn became an addiction. Almost every lunch hour — except on Sundays — found him looking for the usual services or just wanting to talk. He'd take her on shopping trips and buy her whatever she wanted. Once, he even paid to spring Lucky from jail. His obsession turned into a $140,000 habit. He had a fairly lucrative practice, but by July, 1985, the illicit expenses were taking their toll on his practice, his bank account and his marriage. Debts were also mounting. The doctor cut back on the meetings and was considering going cold turkey on Dawn.

After remains of Dr. W. Alan Canty were found near this Emmet County cabin in 1985, police began to unravel a bizarre story of tangled identities — and murder.

Detroit Free Press, July 24, 1988

That didn't sit too well with Lucky. He had a pretty sweet deal and wanted to keep it rolling along. He told Dawn to lure the doctor to their home and talk him into continuing the visits.

When Canty showed up, Dawn went into a bedroom while Lucky stated the case for more Dawn. But words weren't working. Canty said he just couldn't keep up the double life. It was wrecking him.

Lucky wasn't buying it. He picked up a handy baseball bat and laid into the psychiatrist. Dawn heard the blows and came out to find the doctor convulsing on the floor. He died there. Now what?

Lucky ordered Dawn outside. Then he dismembered the body, storing some of it in the freezer and loading the rest into the doctor's black Buick. Lucky had a truck driver friend, and he headed over there and told the guy he had some evidence he needed to bury. Thinking they were bad checks or something relatively tame, the driver gave advice, then offered to come along to help. Imagine his surprise when he found out what they were getting rid of.

A few days later, the two buddies headed north along I-75, tossing body pieces out the window. Two hundred seventy-five miles later, they were down to the head, hands and feet. Those were buried in a field outside Alanson.

After that, Lucky couldn't live up to his name. He was a braggart, and someone talked. He was found guilty of first-degree murder. Dawn Spens served 10 months in jail for helping mutilate the doctor's body. She left the profession, got married and became a mother and substance abuse counselor in Ann Arbor.

Lemons
• • • • • • • •

Judge Michael Sapala, who acquitted Dawn of the murder charges, offered this bit of philosophy when he retired in 2012: "I have what I call the 'lemon theory' of human behavior. There are some lemons out there. No amount of education or faith-based relationships or family will help them. They're just lemons and they're going to do some very bad things. The tough part is to recognize who's a lemon and who isn't. When you find one, they have to be isolated, it's as simple as that."

Blood Ties
• • • • • • • • • •

Canty's father, Alan Canty Sr., was a criminal psychologist who was called on to help police create a profile of the Coed Killer in Ypsilanti and Ann Arbor in the late 1960s (page 108).

MURDER MAP

Dr. Canty had an office at the Fisher Building. The structure was designed by well-known Detroit architect Albert Kahn in the 1920s and is still one of the Motor City's poshest office addresses. Less than a mile west on **West Grand Boulevard** is Hitsville, USA, the house where Motown Records recorded in its glory days of the 1960s.

Canty's forays from the Fisher to the Corridor likely took him down **Cass Avenue**. The road runs through lively sections of Wayne State University campus, past ethnic restaurants and shops catering to students.

Yet in the 1970s and 80s, Cass Corridor was pretty much shorthand in Detroit for whores, drugs and danger.

So what part was the Corridor? It consisted of **Cass Avenue** from **I-75** to the southern end of the Wayne State campus, then from **Woodward** to **M-10/ John C. Lodge Freeway**.

The southern end of the corridor will soon be dominated by the new arena for the Red Wings, a short walk from where the Tigers and Lions play and from the Fox Theatre.

Dawn and the doctor's first "date" was at the Temple Hotel, a seedy husk even then, where rooms were rented by the hour.

Dawn and Lucky lived at an apartment building known as Homewood Manor at **644 Charlotte**, Apartment 202. They later moved to a bungalow at **2518 Casper Street**, southwest of the Corridor. This is where Dr. Canty met his end. Of course, it was the doctor's addiction to Dawn that had allowed them to lease the home in the neighborhood, an improvement over the apartment.

Lucky and his truck driver friend buried Dr. Canty's body parts near the northern Michigan towns of Alanson and Pellston, off **Douglas Lake Road**, where the University of Michigan Biological Research Station is located.

The two towns sit along highway **U.S. 31**, between Petoskey and the Mackinac Bridge. Alanson's downtown faces north, across from hillside gardens exploding with color throughout the summer. Many of the buildings have retained their lumber-era rustic charm. Neighboring Pellston heralds itself as "Icebox of the Nation" because of frequent national record-low temperatures. The Pellston Regional Airport is a source of local pride.

Canty lived in a Tudor-style home in Grosse Pointe Park on **Windmill Drive** with his wife, Jan. For a tour of 20th century auto baron opulence in the Grosse Pointes, take a drive up **East Jefferson Avenue** from Detroit, where it turns to Lake Shore Drive. The wealth of the Fords (but not Henry who stayed in Dearborn), the Dodges and others gravitated here in the form of mansions and yacht clubs.

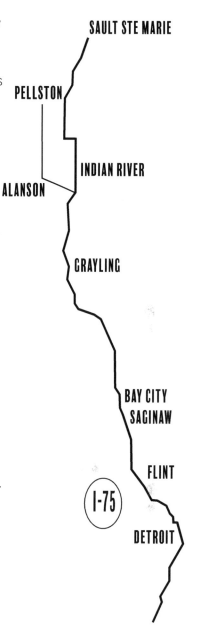

Dr. Canty's body parts were spread along I-75 from Detroit to Indian River. The head, hands and feet were buried in a field near Alanson.

BIG FOOT

THE YEAR: 1976
THE CRIME: MURDER
THE MOTIVE: UNKNOWN

ON A NORMAL DAY, SEX WORKERS STRUGGLE WITH VIOLENCE, DRUG ADDICTION, ALCOHOLISM, DEPRESSION AND DISEASE, BUT IN 1976 THE JOB WAS POSITIVELY TERRIFYING.

A killer was on the loose.

The early, surviving victims described the killer as tall, black, with unusually large feet. That earned him the nickname the "Bigfoot Murderer."

Fear gripped the infamously seedy Cass Corridor, and some women started packing heat. News accounts even quoted that the pimps were upset because the attacks were making their hookers a little too "high strung."

Bigfoot claimed seven victims before the spree ended. Ultimately, he turned out to be every bit as elusive as the legendary creature of the Northwest, also known by the Bigfoot handle. The case remains unsolved.

Bigfoot wasn't Detroit's only serial killer to disappear. Four years later, in 1980, eighteen women were brutally murdered — twelve by strangulation — and all but one were dumped in public outdoor spaces. Two men were arrested, but only one convicted. Thirteen of the murders are still unsolved.

The Sick Golden Years of Serial Murder

During the decade of the 60s, 19 serial murders were reported — more than in all the decades preceding. But something happened in 1970 because over the next ten years, 119 cases of serial murder occurred. Even worse were the 1980s, with 200 reported. In the 90s, the number dropped back to 141, and in the 00s the number was only 61. Although no one can say for sure why serial killing spiked over those three decades, better record-keeping and policing are certainly factors. Overall, crime is way down since the 1980s.

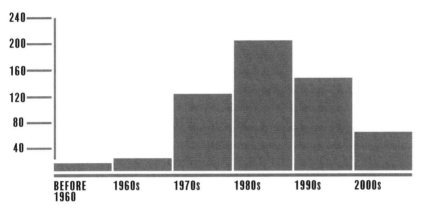

Source: James Alan Fox and Jack Levin, *Extreme Killing: Understanding Serial and Mass Murder*, Sage Publications, 2011

Serial killers Who Were Never Identified or Caught

- **Zodiac:** 5 confirmed dead, 37 claimed by killer, 1969 to 1974, SF Bay Area

- **Highway of Tears killer or killers**: 18 confirmed, over 40 presumed, 1969 to 2006, British Columbia's Highway 16

- **Alphabet Killer:** 3 confirmed, 1971 - 1973, Rochester, NY

- **Freeway Phantom:** 6 confirmed, 1971 to 1972, Washington, D.C.

- **Bigfoot Murderer:** 7 confirmed, 1976, Detroit, MI

- **Redhead Murderer:** 8 confirmed, 1983, Tennessee, Arkansas, Kentucky, Mississippi, Pennsylvania

- **Colonial Parkway Killer:** 8 confirmed, 1986, Virginia

NEW YEAR'S EVIL

THE YEAR: 1971
THE CRIME: MURDER
THE MOTIVE: UNKNOWN

THERE'S NOTHING LIKE SITTING AROUND A MICHIGAN CAMPFIRE, TELLING SPOOKY STORIES.

Remember the ones about the lover's lane? You know the kind: Teen lovers find one of the few places they can get away from the world. It's dark outside, but inside the radio's glowing, playing their favorite song. The windows steam up. As youngsters move in toward each other….

Here's the real story.

Jack Keyes and his girlfriend Kathy Radtke were driving around town in Jack's '67 Mustang on the last evening of 1971. Kathy, a Novi High School honors student, is remembered as wearing purple bell-bottoms and a purple long-sleeved Mickey Mouse t-shirt when they stopped at a garage to see about a car part. Then they briefly visited Jack's parents' home, where family and friends were playing cards. Pretty soon, they said, they'd head over to Kathy's parents' house. Or that was the plan.

But dinnertime came, and Kathy's parents wondered why they weren't there. When the clock struck midnight, they didn't feel like toasting the new year. The kids never made it home.

The next morning, Jack's brother and a friend went looking for them. They checked around to some of their favorite haunts in town. Nothing. They wondered if they might have visited a parking spot for teen couples south of town. They drove out to Napier Road, gravel crunching under their tires. They took the dirt drive in toward the pond that was right next to the Detroit House of Corrections. Jack's Mustang was off the road and down a bank, next to the water.

As they slowly approached the car, they saw Jack reclined in the front seat, alone, shirtless and frozen. He'd been shot twice in the face with a .22. His jacket was folded neatly beneath his head.

The '67 Mustang.

There was no trace of Kathy.

But there was another set of tire tracks, apparently from a four-wheel drive vehicle.

One of the first thoughts from the police, naturally, was the prison next-door. But nobody had broken out, so that wasn't it. Maybe they sat under the moonlight, heard a rustling in the bushes or footsteps approaching, just like in one of those campfire stories. Or maybe they were killed elsewhere and towed to the spot with a chain, which is actually the favored theory the police worked with at the time.

For several weeks, officers questioned dozens of friends and family and acquaintances, and gave lie-detector tests to several. They circulated descriptions of Kathy: 5'11", long brown hair, purple bell-bottoms and moccasins. They checked out Jeeps and other four-wheel drive vehicles in the area that might have been able to tow the Mustang, but to no avail.

In the spring, two boys found Kathy's nude body floating in Crotched Lake, on the other side of Oakland County.

The killer was never identified. Whatever happened, the case has grown colder than a February morning, nearly half a century ago.

MURDER MAP

The spot where Jack and his Mustang were found — off **Napier Road** between **Six Mile** and **Five Mile** roads — is now a pricey subdivision. The pond is still there, but the expensive homes surrounding it give no hint of the ghastly, unsolved mystery.

Northville and Plymouth are western suburbs of Detroit. They are both known for their thriving and toney downtowns skirted by spacious well-maintained homes, many a century or more old.

PEDAL TO THE METAL

THE YEAR: 1989
THE CRIME: MURDER
THE MOTIVE: THE WEIGHT OF THE WORLD

TWENTY-EIGHT-YEAR OLD LAWRENCE DELISLE, MANAGER OF A TIRE STORE, AS DRIVING HIS WIFE AND THEIR FOUR YOUNG CHILDREN HOME ONE AUGUST NIGHT IN 1989.

They'd just bought cookies and were heading east on Eureka Road in Wyandotte.

Just a normal summer drive for a family who'd just moved to a new home in Lincoln Park. Until the leg cramp.

Suddenly, Lawrence's foot jammed down on the gas pedal. The car ran through the intersection at Biddle Road and picked up speed down the narrow stretch of Eureka Road, which dead-ends just before the Detroit River. He'd been complaining of leg cramps lately, his wife Suzanne knew. But he wasn't moving it off the accelerator, and the speedometer needle continued to climb.

Suzanne gaped in horror as the car zoomed toward the river and the thick-timbered barrier in front of it. She reached over and tried to turn off the ignition, change the gears, frantically hoping to save her four children.

The runaway car's engine whined toward the rushing, dirty waters ahead. Wide-eyed, people stood up on the balconies of their apartments and watched helplessly as the Ford LTD crashed through the barrier and plunged into 30 or so feet of water. The windows were open as the car sank, and Suzanne and Lawrence struggled out of the vehicle, instinctively going for that living breath of air. As they rose to the surface, a nearby boater saw them and brought them ashore. Suzanne was hysterical. "I am not leaving without my children! Save my children! They are under water!"

Police scuba divers jumped in. It took an hour to bring up the four children, one-by-one, to the waiting ambulances. At Wyandotte General Hospital, doctors tried desperately to revive them. All four of the children — Bryan, 8; Melissa, 4; Kathryn, 2; and Emily, 8 months, died.

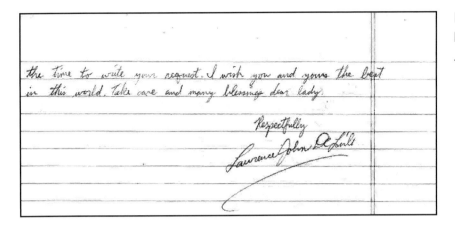

the time to write your request. I wish you and yours the best in this world. Take care and many blessings dear lady.

Respectfully

Lawrence John DeLisle

Last page of the letter written by DeLisle and sent to Roberta Jasina.

For a day or so, Lawrence DeLisle had the sympathy of the world. But something didn't seem quite right. For one thing, witnesses in those balconies along the river were eager to say they'd recognized the car as it zipped past them. They'd seen it before, slowly driving down the dead-end a couple times, stopping when it reached the barrier, as if the driver was casing the joint.

After lengthy questioning by investigators and a lie detector test, Lawrence confessed. He had meant to drown his children.

He was charged with four counts of first degree murder, for the kids, and one count for attempting to murder his wife.

But when the case went to trial, the defense attorney was adamant about Lawrence's innocence. There was no confession, he maintained. Rather, it was a kind of nervous breakdown, a brainwashing brought about by eight hours of brutal interrogation without a lawyer. Also, the car was defective.

The prosecutor disagreed. Lawrence was drowning in debt, burdened by fatherhood, tired of it all. Furthermore, he'd planned to kill himself as well as his family. After all, there was the car.

That's right: the Ford LTD that went in the river was the very car in which his own father had committed suicide less than two years before.

The jury put Lawrence DeLisle away for life.

Now in his 50s and behind bars in the city of Coldwater, he still maintains his innocence. In a handwritten letter to WWJ news anchor Roberta Jasina, he blamed the car and his leg cramp and accused the police of a cover-up. He was "unethically crucified by defamatory media reporting," he wrote.

MURDER MAP

The end of **Eureka Road** overlooking the island/city of Grosse Ile is lined with apartments and condos. At the end of the road is a guardrail, a worn plot of grass, and another fence.

The downriver city of Wyandotte is named after an American Indian tribe of the Huron nation. The city's downtown with its boutiques and galleries is just north of **Eureka Road**, centered on **Biddle Avenue**.

Wyandotte is also home to attractive river walks and parks.

ROBISON FAMILY MASSACRE

THE YEAR: 1968
THE CRIME: MURDER
THE MOTIVE: UNKNOWN

IT WAS THE SUMMER OF 1968, AND THE TIGERS WERE CHIPPING AWAY AT THE AMERICAN LEAGUE ON THEIR WAY TO A WORLD SERIES VICTORY.

The first Big Mac was served in Pittsburgh, Richard Nixon said "Sock it to me" live on TV and the Beatles released their hit "Hey Jude." But amid the excitement, the country was reeling from the assassinations that spring of Martin Luther King Jr. and Bobby Kennedy. Tommie Smith and John Carlos, both medal winners at the Mexico City Olympics, raised their fists on the victory stand to protest deplorable race relations. Speaking of which, Detroit's riots had taken place the year before, while Washington, D.C., Baltimore and Chicago were now experiencing similar violence.

The Robison family — Richard and Shirley and their four kids — seemed to be your classic, upper-middle-class, metro Detroit family, the kind with cottages Up North. No doubt, they were relieved to drive away from the local and national hubbub and head to their quiet summer place on Lake Michigan, north of Petoskey.

The cottage was a classic, middle-class, Michigan waterfront home. Looking at old photos, you can almost hear that inviting smack of a wooden screen door springing shut or feel the breeze coming through the many windows.

This cottage was on a prime-choice site, too. It jutted out on pretty much the easternmost point of that rounded top section of the Lower Peninsula between Petoskey and the Mackinac Bridge. Private and peaceful.

That is, until that idyllic setting was shattered by the sickening smell of six decaying bodies — the entire family. The stench is what first lured neighbors to an unimaginable murder site.

Early on the evening of June 25, police figured, someone sneaked up to the back of the Robison cottage and opened fire with a .22 ArmaLite semi-automatic.

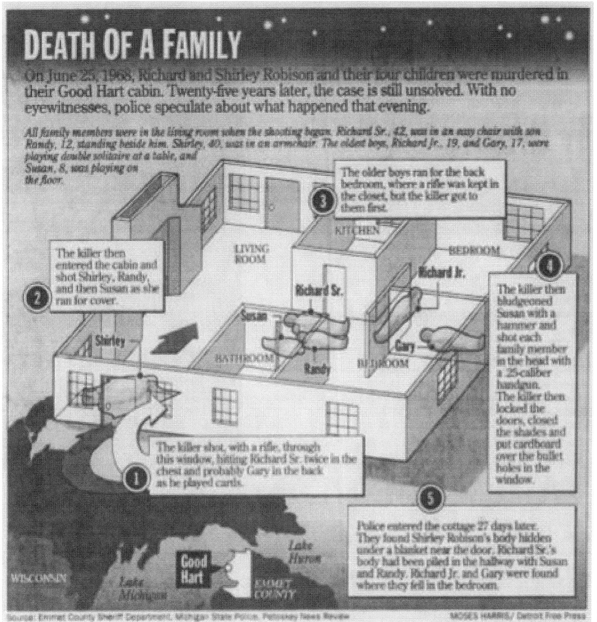

DEATH OF A FAMILY

On June 25, 1968, Richard and Shirley Robison and their four children were murdered in their Good Hart cabin. Twenty-five years later, the case is still unsolved. With no eyewitnesses, police speculate about what happened that evening.

All family members were in the living room when the shooting began. Richard Sr., 42, was in an easy chair with son Randy, 12, standing beside him. Shirley, 40, was in an armchair. The oldest boys, Richard Jr., 19, and Gary, 17, were playing double solitaire at a table, and Susan, 8, was playing on the floor.

3 The older boys ran for the back bedroom, where a rifle was kept in the closet, but the killer got to them first.

2 The killer then entered the cabin and shot Shirley, Randy, and then Susan as she ran for cover.

4 The killer then bludgeoned Susan with a hammer and shot each family member in the head with a .25-caliber handgun. The killer then locked the doors, closed the shades and put cardboard over the bullet holes in the window.

1 The killer shot, with a rifle, through this window, hitting Richard Sr. twice in the chest and probably Gary in the back as he played cards.

5 Police entered the cottage 27 days later. They found Shirley Robison's body hidden under a blanket near the door. Richard Sr.'s body had been piled in the hallway with Susan and Randy. Richard Jr. and Gary were found where they fell in the bedroom.

KITCHEN · LIVING ROOM · BEDROOM · BATHROOM · BEDROOM

Richard Jr. · Richard Sr. · Susan · Randy · Gary · Shirley

WISCONSIN · Lake Michigan · Good Hart · Lake Huron · EMMET COUNTY

Source: Emmet County Sheriff Department, Michigan State Police, Petoskey News Review

MOSES HARRIS / Detroit Free Press

Detroit Free Press, July 4, 1993

The assailant then crashed through the back door and killed every single family member with execution-style pistol shots to the head. The killer stacked the children's bodies on top of the father. The mother's body was displayed to look as if she'd been raped.

June was cooler than usual that year, so the furnace kept running. Add 27 days and the result was horrific.

Only one pair of bloody footprints was discovered in the cabin, and Joseph Scolaro, a young employee at Richard Robison's advertising firm who'd been embezzling from the business's coffers, quickly became the prime suspect.

But evidence was painfully circumstantial. Scolaro had no alibi, but then no one could prove he'd been in northern Michigan either. Scolaro purchased both a .22 ArmaLite and Beretta pistol, but neither weapon was in his possession.

He failed two lie detector tests, but what does that mean? And, the bloody footprints could not be matched. The investigation of Scolaro went on for two years, but in the end the Emmet County prosecutor had to admit he had nothing on him.

A couple years later, a newly elected Oakland County prosecutor decided to reopen the case. The case was out of his jurisdiction, but the victims had lived in the county. Forensics were improving and he thought he'd get a conviction. When Scolaro heard the news, he typed a suicide note, calling himself a liar, a cheat and a phony — but not a murderer. In a handwritten note to his mother, he also claimed his innocence. "I'm sick and scared," it said, "God and everyone, please forgive me." He killed himself on March 8, 1973. He was thirty years old.

Although many have tried, no substantiating evidence has yet been uncovered and the case remains one of the state's most troubling mysteries.

Bringing the House Down

The homes and buildings in many of these horrific tales no longer exist. That's not too surprising since most of us have no desire to go to sleep at night in a place where blood has been shed — or pooled, or dripped or splattered.

Michigan law does not require realtors to go out of their way to tell a customer that a murder has occurred in a home, though many states do. Still, with Google and word of mouth, such things are usually fairly simple to uncover. And chances are pretty good there will be no sale. The value of a house visited by violent death sinks fast.

Many murder-homes have been taken down, perhaps because the owners realized a sale was a lost cause. Even in Detroit, where there are whole blocks of homes missing, there are others where the murder-home is gone yet the rest of the neighborhood is largely intact and well-kept.

And sometimes it goes well beyond a poor return and bad juju. The physical evidence just won't go away. When the Robison family was massacred in their own cabin north of Petoskey, the blood outline of Shirley, the mother, stayed on the floor until it was demolished a few years later.

MURDER MAP

Two-lane scenic highway **M-119** between Harbor Springs and Cross Village is often called the **Tunnel of Trees**. There's hardly a more peaceful or pleasant place to be when the summer sun is a bit too oppressive. Hop in the car, open the sunroof and enjoy a long ride in the shade.

When you see the sign for Good Hart, try not to let a chill crawl up your spine. If you know what happened here in the summer of 1968, that is.

The actual site of the now demolished cabin is north of Good Hart and is among a private enclave of homes.

Old newspaper photo indicating the location of the Benny Evangelist home (see page 13). It is no longer there.

A CONVENIENT CONFESSION

THE YEAR: 1996 – 2015
THE CRIME: MURDER
THE MOTIVE: SILENCING THE VICTIM

GERALDINE MONTGOMERY WAS 68 YEARS OLD WHEN SOMEONE BROKE INTO HER HOME, RAPED HER, THEN STUFFED HER INTO THE TRUNK OF HER CAR.

The rapist became a murderer when he turned on the ignition and left the widow and retired teacher's aide to gasp her last breaths as the car idled and filled her garage with fumes. He left the house with $30 in cash. Montgomery was discovered by her daughter the next morning when church officials called, asking why her mother hadn't shown up to prepare the Sunday communion table. "She would have never left the communion not taken care of, the coffee not taken care of, her Sunday school class not taken care of without having called somebody."

Dozens of area men were rounded up and questioned. Eighteen-year-old Jason Ryan, who'd been staying at a house near Montgomery's was one of many suspects. He submitted to a polygraph test — nothing. Then Jamie Peterson, a twenty-three-year-old who'd already spent years shuttling between psychiatric wards and juvenile group homes, confessed. "Well Dad," he wrote from jail, "I finally made a name for myself like you wanted…. Damn, I must be the best con 'liar' in the world." That Peterson had mental health issues should have rung false-confession alarm bells. It didn't. That DNA evidence found at the scene did not match Peterson should have signaled that the investigation was not over and stopped it from going to trial. It didn't. Jamie Peterson was found guilty and sentenced to life without parole.

Seventeen years went by before lawyers and law students from Ann Arbor and Chicago convinced Kalkaska County prosecutor Michael Perreault to enter the DNA onto a national database. Guess what: It wasn't Peterson, it was Jason Ryan.

Ryan had quite the story, though, about how his DNA could have ended up at Montgomery's home. Sex. That's right, another older woman approached Ryan outside the library, asked for sex, then turned him on to her friend Montgomery. It was totally consensual, his attorney declared. Too bad he couldn't remember the other "older woman's" name or any other details. And it was totally a coincidence that Montgomery was murdered the same day she'd paid for sex.

"It was absolutely preposterous," said a retired teacher who knew Montgomery.

Others agreed that the evidence against Ryan was damning.

So why didn't they find the evidence back in 1996? Many believe that the late prosecutor Brian Donnelly and police were determined to fit the suspect to the crime. At the time, Jamie Peterson seemed eager to grab some notoriety from the murder, for whatever reason, but he didn't always know the details. Often, he gave his interviewers the wrong answers, but changed his mind when they filled him in on the correct details. They even drew a map of the layout of the house for him after his initial answers didn't match the floor plan.

And then there's this from interrogation transcripts regarding a candle investigators had found in a tree across the street:

Police interrogator: How were you seeing when you were in the house and it was dark?

Jamie: What do you mean?

Police: Well, it was dark in the house, how did you see?

Jamie: Lighter.

Police: Did you ever light a candle?

Jamie: Yeah, there was a candle in the living room.

Years later, a neighbor learned of the candle controversy and said it had not even come from Montgomery's house. The neighbor was 13 at the time, and said it was her mother's candle and she had broken it and put it in a tree so she wouldn't get in trouble. Fingerprints on the candle supported her story.

Also, a next-door neighbor said he saw a blond guy through the window of the house on the evening of the murder. Peterson is not blond.

But the real breakthrough was the development of a national, standardized DNA profile database, plus much greater accuracy in testing.

Peterson was cleared of the charges in 2014 and was released to a halfway house in Pontiac. Jason Ryan, who initially walked after tricking a lie detector, was convicted in 2015 by his own genetic fingerprint.

MURDER MAP

Kalkaska grew as a railroad town in the lumbering era. In recent decades, it has seen booms and busts in oil and gas drilling. It sits between Traverse City and Grayling on **M-72**, and between Cadillac and Petoskey on **U.S. 131**. Kalkaska gets a lot of visits from snowmobilers and trout fishing enthusiasts.

Fur, Trees, Labor
•••••••••••••••••

Several Indian tribes inhabited Michigan for 10,000 years or so before Europeans arrived: Chippewa (or Ojibway or Ojibwe), Ottawa (or Odawa), Potawatomi, Sauk, Wyandot (or Huron), among others. All were part of the Algonquian (or Iroquoian) nation to the east. The tribes smelted copper in the Upper Peninsula for tools, weapons and jewelry. They established fishing, hunting and farming communities and trading posts all over what we now call the state of Michigan.

The first European was explorer Étienne Brûlé. Brûlé portaged up the mighty rapids, or sault, which the French would name Sault Ste. Marie, into Lake Superior about the time those pilgrims from England were touching down at Plymouth Rock. The Frenchman's death could almost be a chapter in this book, except that it happened in what is now Ontario. It is believed that Huron Indians suspected him of a double-cross, so they killed and cannibalized him.

His explorations ushered in the fur-trading era. French trappers learned Native American canoe-building skills and spread out among Great Lakes' tributary rivers in search of beaver dams. The famously busy rodent had the misfortune of growing silky, water-resistant coats that quickly became a must-have for hats back in Paris. Hence, fur was the first major industry to draw a wave of immigrants onto the two peninsulas.

Next came the lumber boom. Maine and other northeastern regions had been pretty much wiped clean of the tall, majestic white pines like those that still covered much of Michigan. The hunger for timber to build an ambitious nation was insatiable and left behind millions of stumps. Some of the towns were as transient as the lumberjacks, who followed the industry wherever there were trees to harvest. Now, the only place in Michigan where you can experience the awe and solitude of Michigan's virgin white pine forests before the boom is at Hartwick Pines State Park near Grayling.

Farmers arrived next, and they removed the stumps — farm by farm — to build the state's agriculture industry.

The industry of the 20th century, of course, was largely automotive. Still, other enterprises — like furniture in Grand Rapids, mining in the Upper Peninsula and turning the farmers' products into things like breakfast cereal in Battle Creek and baby food in Fremont — flourished around the state.

All of these industries waxed and waned. And always, always, there were people who just didn't get along....

WE'RE NOT PLAYING ANYMORE

THE YEAR: 1763
THE CRIME: MURDER
THE MOTIVE: WAR

A GAME OF LACROSSE SEEMED LIKE A FITTING DIVERSION ON AN UNUSUALLY WARM SPRING DAY.

There certainly wasn't much else to entertain the British soldiers at the passage between lakes Michigan and Huron. It had been fairly quiet at Fort Michilimackinac since the Brits had won its control from the French and the American Indians a couple of years earlier.

The game was to be between the Ojibwe and the Sauk Indians. Lacrosse had a 1,000-year history among Native Americans, and players numbered up to 1,000 — for each team! Fort commander Major George Etherington gave the game the go-ahead despite warnings. He was sick of hearing rumors of Native uprisings and announced that the next warmongerer would get sent to the lock-up in Fort Detroit. Major Etherington relaxed and placed a bet on the Ojibwe. Returning the favor, the Ojibwe invited him and his garrison to the sidelines outside the fort. Now, the doors were open, weapons abandoned — let the game begin.

In more ways than one, this wasn't the lacrosse we know now, but an ancestor of the game that's growing more and more popular on college campuses. The original was far rougher, lasted longer — two or three days — and was played in honor of the Creator. But like today, athletes lofted a ball to and from the netted pockets at the ends of their sticks. They collided and knocked each other down as they fought for the ball.

The game was officially declared open in honor of the British king's birthday. Five hundred players and hundreds more fans looked on. In the early June heat, the keepers of the fort sweated in their uniforms, but not as much as the Native women wrapped in bulky blankets.

Mohawk Nation lacrosse champions in 1869.

Then, like a baseball over a neighbor's fence, the game ball sailed over the wall of the fort.

That was the sign. Steel-bladed knives and tomahawks — many of which they'd just bought from the British with furs — came out of women's blankets and other hiding places.

Lacrosse players from both sides plus the Native spectators rushed into the fort, using the surprise to overtake the British soldiers in hand-to-hand combat. Many were slashed or stabbed in the initial attack. Twenty-seven of the original 35 died.

A trader wrote in his diary: "Going instantly to my window I saw a crowd of Indians within the fort furiously cutting down every Englishman they found."

A few prisoners were taken that day, including Major Etherington. Tribal officials spared the major's life due to friendship, and probably the hopes of a rich ransom.

The Ojibwe held the fort for a year before the British took it back.

MURDER MAP

The site is now part of Mackinac State Historic Parks.

The fort has been reconstructed based on archaeological finds there. Costumed re-enactors demonstrate crafts and weapons from the period.

In order to be fully immersed in that era, you may want to face away from the Mackinac Bridge looming overhead, which wasn't there until almost 200 years later.

SALEM ON THE STRAITS

THE YEAR: LATE 1700s – EARLY 1800s
THE CRIME: WAR
THE MOTIVE: CLEANSING THE WORLD OF SINNERS

WHEN THE 1700s TURNED INTO THE 1800s, MACKINAC ISLAND WAS A STRATEGIC WATCH-POINT HELD BY THE BRITISH.

From there, they controlled the Straits of Mackinac, a busy waterway for the fur trade and military adventures. Fort Mackinac, high atop a south-facing hill, kept its cannons trained on the ships sailing between lakes Huron, Michigan and Superior.

With all those soldiers and sailors coming and going, brothels and purveyors of spirits did a booming business. But the puritan element in the town turned up their noses at the ladies of the evening. These brazen hussies were not only corrupting the wilderness-dwelling fur trappers and fort soldiers, they were tempting the upstanding pillars of the civilian population.

It's a very short step from wench to witch, and those "upstanding pillars" were happy to take it.

Mackinac Island's unlucky ones were singled out to take a forced dip in the cold water of a deep lagoon on the southeast end of the island. Weighed down with rocks, they were tossed off the twenty-foot drop-off. If they rose to the top to save themselves, they were guilty. If not, well, they died innocent. Seven women lost their lives to the cruel, no-win test.

The spot is now referred to as the Drowning Pool, and some say it's haunted. The pool is located among the waterfront lawns and Adirondack chairs of the Mission Point Resort. Legends of mysterious shadows rising off the surface and inexplicably huge splashes have long attracted ghost enthusiasts and paranormal investigators.

Cooling Down Wicked Women

The concept of ordeal by water is an old one, going back further than the Bible. For witch hunts of the 16th and 17th centuries it was the "in" thing to do. French travel writer Francois Maximilian Misson has a rather mechanical description of an English practice in the era of Queen Elizabeth I:

"The way of punishing scolding women is pleasant enough. They fasten an armchair to the end of two beams twelve or fifteen feet long, and parallel to each other, so that these two pieces of wood with their two ends embrace the chair, which hangs between them by a sort of axle, by which means it plays freely, and always remains in the natural horizontal position in which a chair should be, that a person may sit conveniently in it, whether you raise it or let it down. They set up a post on the bank of a pond or river, and over this post they lay, almost in equilibrio, the two pieces of wood, at one end of which the chair hangs just over the water. They place the woman in this chair and so plunge her into the water as often as the sentence directs, in order to cool her immoderate heat."

In the Land of Silent C's

Two forts, for awhile, served the same purpose for the British. Michilimackinac in present-day Mackinaw City was there first. The French built it as a hub of the booming fur trapping industry, and the British won it over during the French and Indian War.

After a few years, though, it was considered too vulnerable to serve its purpose. For one thing, it was made of wood, which burns, and it was also much too close to the shore, and therefore easy to invade. So, during the Revolutionary War, the Brits built the new, stone fort high on a hill on nearby Mackinac Island. They dropped the Michili- part of the name, and just went with Fort Mackinac.

Note: If you're not from the area, you may make the mistake of saying "MACK-in-ack." Really, Mackinaw City is the only of the Mackinacs that is spelled the way it sounds in English. All the others — the Straits, the Bridge, the Island — are pronounced Mackinaw even though they end in c. Same goes for Fort Michilimackinac.

HUMAN PELTS

THE YEAR: 1775
THE CRIME: MURDER
THE MOTIVE: PROOF OF PURCHASE

DID HE OR DIDN'T HE? ONLY HIS HAIR COLLECTORS KNOW FOR SURE.

General Henry Hamilton was a British official at Fort Detroit during the Revolutionary War who had a bloody reputation. He is said to have paid Natives and French Canadians for the scalps of white American settlers.

The fort was a distant outpost in the 1770s that got its marching orders from the King's officials in Quebec. Hamilton arrived in 1775, just after the war started. He was a civilian lieutenant governor, as well as Superintendent of Indian Affairs, and was pretty good at negotiating with the Natives. He may have even admired them, as he sketched a great many of their portraits during his four-year stint.

That affinity came into play when officials ordered Hamilton to send out native troops to raid American pioneers in Virginia, Pennsylvania and Kentucky in 1777. The British had decided not to use Native forces in the main war out East. However, they figured they could use them to keep the colonists from pushing the frontier too far west of the Appalachian Mountains. That way, it wouldn't even look like it was the British murdering civilians.

But the attackers killed and scalped hundreds of pioneers. Colonists believed that Hamilton, up in Fort Detroit, was paying a bounty for the war souvenirs and began calling him "General Hair-Buyer."

A year later, Hamilton was ordered to Illinois to take back an outpost at Vincennes. The Americans captured him. Because of the raids, he was declared a war criminal rather than a prisoner and was placed in chains. He spent two years in irons before Thomas Jefferson granted him parole.

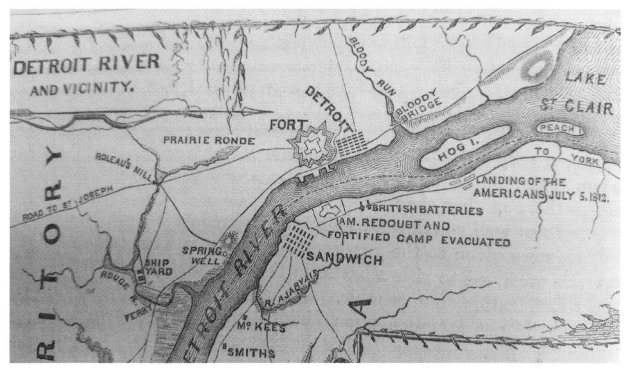

Location of Fort Detroit.

Scalping

The act of scalping, or the cutting of human hair with part of the scalp to display as a war trophy, is as old as the hills and not restricted to Native Americans. In fact, tribes west of the Mississippi River did not practice it.

Reports of scalping go back as far as the Father of History, Herodotus, who lived 484–425 BC and wrote about things much older. It continued into medieval times, and the ancient Germans were adept.

In western Africa, more than 700 human pelts were displayed in the Kingdom of Dahomey (present-day Benin), supposedly all captured by a single group of female warriors, which may be the origin of the legend of the Amazons.

In the United States, colonial governments were not immune, ordering out for their own trophies of war. During King George's War (1689), for instance, Massachusetts governor William Shirley offered a bounty for scalps acquired from supporters of the French. The order included the scalps of children.

COED KILLER

THE YEAR: 1967 – 1969
THE CRIME: MURDER
THE MOTIVE: HATRED OF WOMEN

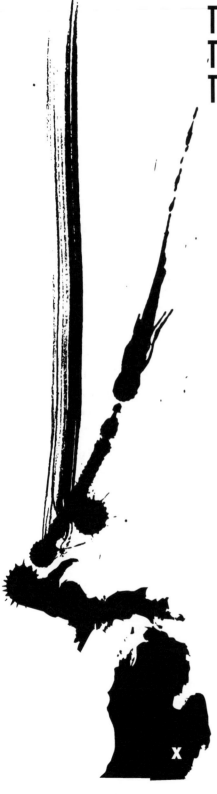

THE KILLING SPREE STARTED IN JULY, 1967, WHEN A BLUE-GRAY CAR FROM THE GENERAL MOTORS LINE PULLED UP TO THE CURB.

Someone watching from a neighboring house saw Mary Terese Fleszar, an Eastern Michigan University accounting student, shake her head no to the driver, then bound up the steps to her apartment building. That's the last she was seen alive. A month later, her badly decayed body was found on abandoned farmland in Dixboro. She'd been stabbed 30 times.

But there was something else: her body had been moved twice, just a few feet each time. It was as if someone had dragged or carried her. Someone who'd found her or someone who knew exactly where she was and had come back to check on her.

Could it get any creepier? After the body was discovered and removed to a funeral home, a young man in a blue-gray Chevy showed up, asking permission to take pictures of the body. He said he was a relative and that the family wanted the photos. No way, said the undertakers. They eventually told police, but unfortunately couldn't give a very good description of the morbid young man.

Of course, it's fairly certain now that the stalker in the car outside Mary's apartment and the morbid photographer were the same man. We also know that he had a thing about returning to the scene of the crime, which was how the police finally arrested him. But back then, the police were simply hoping and praying that Mary's murder was an isolated case.

No such answered prayers. A year later, another EMU student, Joan Elspeth Schell, disappeared while hitchhiking. Her nude body showed up in an Ann Arbor ditch with her miniskirt around her neck. The young man in the Chevy was actually questioned after this second murder. He had been seen with the victim before her disappearance. Yet he was cleared because he said he was with his mother at the time of the crime. Police detectives did not follow up.

Photo collage of five of the six women killed.

Ann Arbor News, June 10, 1969

Nine months went by without a peep, and then the murders resumed with a vengeance.

On March 21, 1969, Jane Louise Mixer, a University of Michigan law student, was found in the Denton Cemetery on top of a grave, her copy of *Catch-22* by her side. The victim had posted on a bulletin board, asking for a ride home to Muskegon.

Four days later, on March 25, the body of 16-year-old high school dropout Maralynn Skelton was found in a subdivision very near where the second victim had been found.

A couple of weeks later, Dawn Basom, thirteen years old and a middle school student, was dumped on the side of an Ypsilanti road.

Then, in June, Alice Elizabeth Kalom, a grad student from U-M, was found in a field near North Territorial Road.

And on July 26, the body of the final victim, Karen Sue Beineman, was found along the Huron River parkway, just outside of Ypsi.

(A01) ANN ARBOR,MICH. AUG 28, 1970: JOHN NORMAN COLLINS sentenced to life in prison smiles at his mother this morning after leaving court. His mother called out to him "good luck and keep your chin up.

Ann Arbor News, January 14, 1977

By this point — in fact, following the death of Dawn Basom — the police, the press and the public started linking the killings, figuring there was one murderer who would probably continue to target young women. And although more than 1,000 convicted sex offenders were investigated, they'd all been eliminated as suspects. The public was absolutely frantic. College students and parents wanted answers, sales of tear gas and knives skyrocketed, no one was hitchhiking anymore.

Fortunately, the police had a plan, and it had to do with keeping the last murder a secret. They'd tried to keep wraps on the previous two murders as well, but the press was keeping pretty close tabs on their police scanners. The cops were finally able to respond to one and keep it off the media's radar, so to speak.

The thing was, there were similarities among many of the victims: They were all brunettes, and most were strangled. There were articles of clothing found around their necks, and cloth was crammed down their throats to quiet them.

August 28, 1970.

John Norman Collins smiles at his mother after sentencing. His last words to her in the free world were, "good luck and keep your chin up."

The blue-gray car or a motorcycle played into several cases. And for some reason, it appeared that all the murders occurred during rainy weather. Yet it was the knowledge that the serial killer returned to some of the bodies that proved most useful of all.

The plan was this: After the cops quietly shipped the last victim to the morgue, they replaced her body with a JCPenney store mannequin. Then, they staked out the area.

It didn't take long. Around midnight, they spotted a guy looking around and sneaking up to the ditch. After spotting the mannequin and sensing that he was being watched, he ran. The police, confounded by rain and mosquitoes, chased after him, but they lost him in the woods.

Luckily though, a break was just around the corner. A security officer at EMU said he'd seen a young guy in a striped shirt tooling around campus on a motorcycle the day Beineman disappeared. Then, employees of a wig shop — the last to see the victim alive — said she'd been there and left with a guy on a motorcycle wearing a striped shirt. The security officer identified the biker as student John Norman Collins.

So Collins became the prime suspect, but police needed more evidence.

Here comes lucky break number two. Collins' uncle invited him to house-sit during a vacation and the uncle was puzzled when he returned to find an area of his basement floor painted black. It just so happened that this uncle was State Police Trooper David Leik.

Leik had his colleagues check out the black paint. After painstakingly scraping, they found something red underneath. While that turned out to be nothing but varnish, they did find blood elsewhere in the basement, and it was the same blood type as the latest victim. DNA testing didn't exist yet, but matching blood types at least narrowed the field of whose blood it could be.

Officially, the only murder that was actually solved was the last one — that of Karen Sue Beineman. It was the prosecutors' strongest case, so that's the one they focused on. It was enough to convict John Norman Collins and sentence him to life in prison.

Collins is currently approaching his 70s as an inmate of Marquette State Prison. He has never admitted to any of the murders.

Last Seen Alive

Karen Sue Beineman, the last time she was seen alive, was heard to say she'd done two stupid things that day: she'd bought a wig, and she'd accepted a ride from a stranger on a motorcycle. Sure, she was a little nervous about the ride...she had the shopkeeper come out and take a look at him...but she went. Not before remarking, hauntingly, "I've got to be either the bravest or the dumbest girl alive, because I've just accepted a ride from this guy." The shopkeeper was later able to identify John Norman Collins from police photographs.

The Serial Count

Is it fair to lump all these murders together and talk about Collins as a serial killer, even though he was only convicted of the one?

Well, for one thing, the killings did stop after he was arrested.

There are other factors, too. Like this: two days before his arrest, a couple of rogue officers went to his house to question him, without the blessing of their superiors. That tipped him off that the heat was on, and Collins got nervous. He quickly gathered up a box of stuff, his trophies, while his roommate watched. Clearly visible in the box was a purse and a purple, high-heeled shoe. (One of the victims was wearing a purple pump when her body was found, but its mate was missing.)

And there was a piece of a belt found in his car that matched one tied around the neck of a 17-year-old California girl murdered in 1969. She had disappeared at a time when Collins was known to have been visiting the Golden State. Her friends said she'd been hanging with a Michigan guy named John, who drove a motorcycle.

So add one from another state to the total, and his likely death toll stands at eight, right? Hold on a minute.

The one case that didn't seem to fit was that of Jane Mixer, the student who posted on a bulletin board for a ride home. She was not found in the same area as the rest. Her body was fully clothed. She was shot rather than stabbed or strangled and had not been sexually molested. More than three decades later, after DNA science made it possible, authorities tested some evidence that had been found on her pantyhose. They ran it through the FBI database and found a match. In 2005, Gary Leiterman was convicted in her death.

But investigators are pretty sure that the killer of the other seven women — six in Michigan and one in California — is sitting in a prison in the Upper Peninsula.

Marquette State Prison.

MURDER MAP

You'll hear people talking about Ann Arbor–Ypsi now and then, since they are next-door neighbors.

Ann Arbor is the bustling, artistic city best known as the home of University of Michigan, a world-class education and research institution. The campus is largely incorporated into the town itself, so that student traffic keeps the city's feel young and lively.

Ypsilanti is the grittier of the two, and is the home of Eastern Michigan University. The campus is more removed from the downtown, so it's struggled a bit more over the years. Among the attractions there is the refurbished and busy Depot Town, a collection of shops, restaurants, and brew pubs in 150-year-old buildings.

Collins lived at **619 Emmet Street** in Ypsilanti, a block south of the campus's Pease Auditorium. He grew up at **7327 Helen Street** in Center Line. Helen is a street of comfortable, brick suburban homes on narrow but deep lots.

"ANGEL OF DEATH"

THE YEAR: 1990
THE CRIME: MURDER
THE MOTIVE: HITTING A LICK

EIGHTEEN-YEAR-OLD TAMARA MARIE MARSHALL WAS A QUIET, PRETTY TEENAGER WHOSE FRIENDS CALLED HER HONEY.

Beneath her sweet facade, however, beat the cold heart of a killer. She often carried a gun, and she and her family members were no strangers to the police.

On April 4, 1990, she was definitely carrying a gun and had plans to use it. Her boyfriend, Marc Caison, picked her up in Southfield and drove to a friend's house. Mark Bell and Jamal Biggs were waiting for them. Talk got to money — the lack of it — and Tamara had an idea. "Let's go hit a lick," she said. That was slang for pulling off an armed robbery. She seemed to think Steve Owens might be a good mark. He was a crack dealer who had lots of cash and dope lying around.

In fact, she'd recently dated the 32-year-old Owens, but they'd had a falling out and he was now dating someone else. When Tamara, alone, walked up to the porch of the St. Aubins house, Owens and his new girlfriend, Janet, were just coming home to change their clothes. They planned to go roller-skating that evening.

Neither Owens nor Janet seemed particularly surprised to see Tamara. Janet even left the old lovers chatting on the front porch while she headed upstairs to watch a video and chill. Two other people (ages 21 and 16) were in the house, relaxing as well.

Tamara and Owens ended their porch conference and Owens figured that was that. He didn't know she was sneaking around the corner to get Bell and Biggs, both armed with .25-caliber pistols. The three of them then headed back to the St. Aubin house and Tamara pounded on the door, yelling for Owens. He bounded back down the stairs, annoyed. When he opened the door, annoyance gave way to shock as Tamara and company forced their way in, demanding cash and drugs.

Detroit Free Press, April 10, 1990

JOHN COLLIER/Detroit Free Press

Upstairs, Janet didn't notice a thing until Tamara walked in and pulled the gun on her. Even then, Janet thought it was a joke. Tamara corrected her.

"You must think you're really bad. You don't think I'll really shoot you," she said, then grabbed Janet's purse and shoved her down the stairs.

On the main floor, the three unlucky friends were lined up against the wall. Biggs and Bell stood over them, yelling at them to empty their pockets and hand over their jewelry. Tamara allowed Janet to keep her earrings. (She wore them to court later, when she testified against the teenager.)

Then, everything went wrong — if it could get any more wrong. For one, people kept coming to the door, walking in, looking for dope or just to chill. Biggs got rid of them, but decided that the hostages needed to get out of sight. Upstairs they all went, where they were made to lie down on the floors of three bedrooms. As far as Janet was concerned, Tamara had exhausted her good will. "Go ahead and kill her," she was reported as saying. "I don't know her."

Bell was curious, however, and asked how old she was. "Fourteen," the girlfriend lied. Bell kicked Owens in the head for dating such a baby. A lot of running up and down the stairs ensued, and then the shots started, punctuated by the sobs and pleas of soon-to-be victims. There were seven shots in all.

Owens got three of the bullets all for himself, but all four were dead.

But more teenagers were coming in the house, "just to be over there…tripping out…capping jokes, having fun." Biggs grabbed one and dragged him down the basement stairs. Bang.

Janet, alone and still alive upstairs, heard Tamara urge the others to get going, to get out. By the time she and the three others sped away, six people lay dead with blood pooling around their heads, and Tamara had earned the nickname "Angel of Death." It clings to her today as she lives out her life in prison without parole.

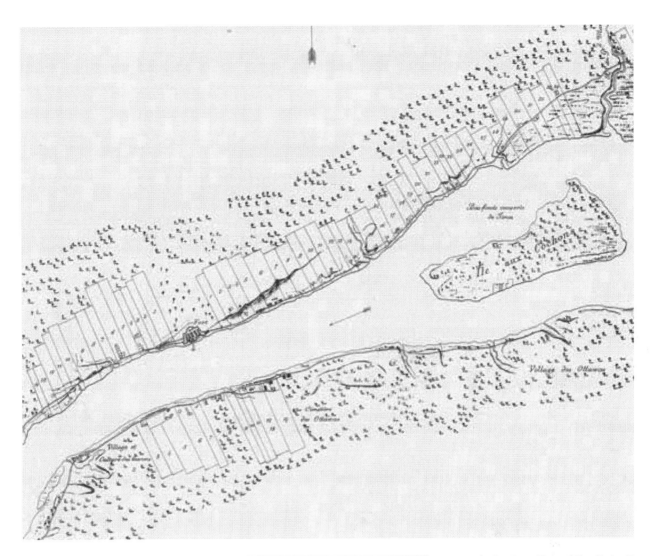

A chart section of the Detroit River and the ribbon farms, made for self-proclaimed Emperor of the French, Napoleon Bonaparte, in 1796.

MURDER MAP

Tamara led the massacre at **17850 St Aubin** — the same street as the murder of the Evangelista family, but about six miles further north.

St. Aubin Street, east of downtown, runs from the Detroit River north through Hamtramck. It was once the site of a farm owned by the St. Aubin family, who traced their roots to a region in France that shared their last name. After French explorer Antoine de la Mothe Cadillac founded Fort Pontchartrain du Détroit in 1701, he granted "ribbon farms" north of the fort. They were called that because they were long, narrow strips of land, 250 feet wide and up to three miles long. Several were owned by members of the St. Aubin family. The family farmed the ribbons for generations until the last of them, Louis St. Aubin, died in 1895.

EASTER'S ALAMO

THE YEAR: 1987
THE CRIME: MURDER
THE MOTIVE: HITTING ROCK BOTTOM

ALBERTA EASTER AND HER THREE SONS WORE EXPENSIVE CLOTHES AND WERE CONSTANTLY ON THE LOOKOUT FOR MONEY-MAKING SCHEMES, LEGAL OR NOT.

They talked big and loved it when people saw them as high-rollers.

In the 70s, they'd started Gold Soul recording studio. Motown had left by then, gone to Los Angeles with founder Berry Gordy, and maybe they thought they'd reign supreme. They recorded some commercial jingles, but Motown they were not.

The late 80s found the four of them — Alberta now 70 years old — living low in the Bungalow Motel on a busy section of Michigan Avenue.

It was a $286 check for a car from Rent-A-Jalopy that graduated them from hucksters to murderers one hot, sticky July night in Inkster.

Two policemen, Clay Hoover and Daniel Dubiel, knocked on the door of one of their adjoining rooms late in the afternoon, as rush hour traffic hummed by outside. They had an arrest warrant for Alberta and her son George Lemons for that $286 check and another written on a closed account.

Easter and her three middleaged sons argued with the officers and showed them they were well-armed. The two policemen called for backup.

When Sergeant Ira Parker arrived, the three officers resumed negotiations. The Easters opened their doors and let them in.

Just after that, the manager and some of the other tenants heard shots fired. The manager ran out yelling, "Are you crazy?" He dove back inside after a bullet whizzed by him.

More police arrived. They trained their rifles on the rooms and pleaded with the family to free the officers and turn themselves in. The family refused and hunkered down.

Intense negotiations continued throughout the night, punctuated by hundreds of rounds fired from the Easters. People in neighboring rooms were trapped under beds, as occasional bullets ricocheted outside or hit windows. The police tried tear gas, but the Easters were prepared and donned their masks.

The stand-off lasted 10 tense, sweaty hours.

Then, about three in the morning, Alberta and sons knew they were beat and came out with their hands up.

Police hoped to find their colleagues tied up with mouths duct-taped. Instead, they found a mound of mattresses and blankets on the floor, oozing blood. Underneath were the three uniformed and bullet-ridden bodies.

Alberta Easter and her sons George, Roy and William Lemons, were sentenced to life in prison. Alberta and George both died behind bars, Alberta in 2011 and George in 1996.

RICHARD LEE/Detroit Free Press

Alberta Easter, wearing shackles on her wrists and ankles and dressed in a white quilted jail-issued shift, is escorted to her arraignment at the Wayne County Circuit Court complex in Westland on Saturday.

Detroit Free Press, July 12, 1987

MURDER MAP

The Bungalow Motel was at **28525 Michigan Avenue,** in Inkster, near a row of modest motels.

EDDIE JEFFERSON STEPS OUT

THE YEAR: 1979
THE CRIME: MURDER
THE MOTIVE: A WOMAN SCORNED

THE HISTORY OF BAKER'S KEYBOARD LOUNGE HAS BEEN MOSTLY UPBEAT.

The favorite haunt of local jazz lovers had, in its glory days, played host to the likes of Ella Fitzgerald, Dave Brubeck and Miles Davis.

Singer Eddie Jefferson's career was on the rise when he played there in 1979. After decades in the tough business of jazz, Eddie had hitched up with young saxophonist Richie Cole. Together, they were recording what would be regarded by many as Eddie's best tracks. Eddie had also recently played at the White House for President Jimmy Carter, and at a packed Carnegie Hall with Sarah Vaughan. That February, Detroit Mayor Coleman Young had presented Eddie with a key to the city.

In May of that year, Eddie chose to open his nationwide tour at Baker's. The house was packed, and the event even attracted some minor glitterati from Hollywood, such as Brenda Vaccaro of "Midnight Cowboy" fame. Yet club owner Clarence Baker said the singer seemed a bit preoccupied and cut his performance short. Later, it begged the question: was Eddie expecting something or someone ominous?

At about 1:30 in the morning, Eddie stepped out the front door of the club with his manager and Richie Cole. They were about to get into a waiting car when Eddie said, "What's that? Some car backfiring?"

Bang, bang. A green Lincoln Continental screeched into action, and a man with a large afro leaned out the passenger window, firing four shots at the singer. The third shot found its mark. Eddie staggered halfway down an alley and collapsed.

Later that night, police arrested a suspect who pointed them in the direction of a tap dancer. She'd known Eddie from the 60s and had been trying to get work with him ever since.

None of the charges stuck in court, however, and the tap dancer skated. No other suspects have ever been named.

Eddie Jefferson had an affable, memorable voice. There was a nasality to his delivery that gave it an irreverent edge. His biggest claim to jazz history, though, is a singing style known as "vocalese". That's where a singer puts words to some of jazz's fastest melodies, originally written for instrumentals. Not the biggest sub-genre going, but it's something. He's known for his vocal treatment of Miles Davis's "So What", and had jazz hits with "Parker's Mood" and "Filthy McNasty." He inspired later jazz artists like Al Jarreau and Manhattan Transfer.

MURDER MAP

Baker's Keyboard Lounge, at **20510 Livernois Avenue**, claims to be the world's oldest operating jazz club. Baker's opened in 1933 as a sandwich restaurant and began booking jazz pianists the following year. The curved-keyboard bar and a small adjoining room are perfect spaces to fill with the sounds of a wailing sax solo or an intimate, blues piano riff.

Baker's got its art deco makeover after it had already been open about 20 years. That was shortly before another jazz legend, pianist Art Tatum, made his last public appearance there in 1956.

It's looking a bit rundown now, and recognizable names are mostly absent from their coming lineup. But then again, there aren't a lot of recognizable jazz names still living.

Clubbing
• • • • • • • • •

In 1986, Baker's was designated a Historic Site by the Michigan State Historic Preservation Office. The club still displays its original price list from 1934 — 26 cents for a beer!

LABOR FORCE

THE YEAR: 1932
THE CRIME: MURDER
THE MOTIVE: GO HOME

THREE YEARS INTO THE GREAT DEPRESSION, DETROIT WAS REELING.

Auto production was down to a quarter of what it had been in the 1920s, and that meant mass layoffs and severe unemployment. Wages for those who hung onto their assembly line jobs were slashed.

Hunger, frustration and bitterness overtook the city. Thousands who'd made the trip across oceans or up from the South to work and live the good life were now scraping to get by. The Unemployed Councils, a nationwide group affiliated with the Communist Party, saw the increasing hopelessness as an opportunity to organize for their brand. A march was planned for the unemployed, and about 3,000 or so showed up. Hardly any of them were Communists, they were simply folks who felt let down by Ford Motor Company and the economy that had crashed around them.

The march took place on a bone-chilling, blustery day in March on Detroit's west side. They intended to march along the Rouge River, through Dearborn, to Ford's largest factory, the mammoth Rouge Plant.

The marchers passed peacefully through Detroit, as the mayor had okayed the demonstration. But when the group reached the city limits, around Miller Road and Fort Street, the Dearborn police fired a wall of tear gas to keep them out of town. Then, one officer fired his gun into the crowd. The protesters began to throw rocks and firefighters retaliated, blasting the marchers with their high-powered water hoses — a fierce weapon even on a warm day.

In the ensuing chaos, hundreds of workers dispersed and then re-grouped further inside Dearborn at the Ford factory. That's when police and Ford's company guards opened fire. Four people died then and there. A fifth lingered for a few weeks before his wounds killed him. Another 22 were injured.

Early newspaper accounts said the protesters started the gunfight and that four policemen were killed. Within a couple days, however, they corrected the information and printed editorials criticizing the conduct of the police and hired guards. What started out as the Ford Hunger March is now remembered as the Ford Massacre.

Less Deadly Forces

In 1937, just five years later, on a pedestrian overpass at the Rouge Plant's No. 4 gate on Miller Road, violence broke out again. This time, United Auto Worker leaders and some of the rank-and-file planned to protest at the afternoon shift change, seeking a raise from $6 a day to $8 a day.

Ford's overzealous security team takes the blame for this one as well. Not only were they mean, but they lacked any public-relations savvy. Right as union leader Walter Reuther and his colleagues were posing for a Detroit News photographer, the guards got out their clubs and beat, stomped and kicked the union men, including Reuther, who they also tossed down two flights of stairs.

There weren't any deaths this time, but one of the union organizers did suffer a broken back.

Also in 1937, Flint General Motors workers staged a sit-down strike for 44 days. The idea was to occupy a plant so non-union workers couldn't come in. Nobody was hurt in that one, either.

And in Grand Rapids, a strike in 1911 by non-union workers in 50 furniture plants turned violent. The strike had already gone on for nearly a month when the John Widdicomb Co. owners tried to get the strikebreakers past the 1,200 or so protesters gathered near the entrance on Fifth Street NW. The strikers pelted cars trying to enter with rocks. There were no deaths in this conflict.

THE WIDOW MAKER

THE YEAR: 1913
THE CRIME: MURDER
THE MOTIVE: PICKING A FIGHT

BARELY A MONTH INTO THE BITTER STRIKE AGAINST THE CALUMET & HECLA MINING COMPANY, A DISTINCT BITTERNESS WAS SETTLING INTO THE FLINTY HILLS OF THE KEWEENAW PENINSULA.

On the one side were the mostly recent immigrants, looking for safer work conditions. On the other were the mine owners, trying to hold down their costs. It got bloody when guards sprayed bullets into a rickety boarding house in Seeberville, south of Houghton.

The miners were under the thumbs of their employers, both at work and at home. Calumet & Hecla — the largest copper producer in the world in the late 1800s — owned its workers' houses, the stores where they spent their wages and the hospitals where they were sent after mining accidents. Workers frequently climbed out of the dark, dank mine shafts 12 hours after they went in, missing the sun for days at a time in the winter.

The strikers were seeking at least $3 a day for all workers. They'd also joined a nationwide movement to regulate the use of child laborers.

But one of their main demands was to end a company cost-saving practice that miners said made a dangerous job downright deadly. It had to do with the two-man drill becoming the one-man drill. If a single worker, they said, was drilling holes in a wall of a remote cave and accidentally caused an avalanche, there'd be nobody to seek help. Even with two people, the job had earned the name "The Widow Maker" from the miners.

So they went on strike on July 23, 1913. After less than a month, tensions were boiling over. The mining companies' security guards were ordered to keep all strikers off company property. When 10 strikers gathered in a park to drink beer within sight of Calumet & Hecla guards, the two groups kept a keen and suspicious eye on each other.

Then, heading home, the miners defiantly cut across company property as threats and insults were exchanged. The guards followed the men, billy clubs at the ready in case of a fight.

They got a fight at the cramped Seeberville boarding house, with wall to wall beds for seventeen. Guards tried to arrest the men without a warrant. One of the strikers was beaten with clubs. A striker then threw a bowling pin at the guards. One guard fired. And that let loose the avalanche of bullets.

Breaking glass and splintering wood, the guards hit two men, both Croatian immigrants. One of them died the next day. Neither had any relationship to the defiant miners the guards were there to arrest.

The victims had not been particularly well known, but they became an instant symbol of defiance in the labor struggle and 5,000 mourners showed up at their funeral. The killings themselves became a rallying cry in the strike that tore apart Calumet and nearby communities, setting the stage for the Italian Hall disaster later that year.

MURDER MAP

A century ago, Seeberville was one of several settlements made of worker houses owned by the copper mining companies. It's now known as Painesdale, a tiny burg a few miles south of Houghton on **M-26.**

ALL THE LITTLE CHILDREN

THE YEAR: 1913
THE CRIME: MURDER
THE MOTIVE: STRIKE-BREAKING (SUSPECTED)

WALK THROUGH CALUMET AND IT FEELS FROZEN IN TIME.

It might not be fair to call it a ghost town, because there are still businesses there and it's home to 700 people. But the place has that just-left feeling of other U.P. towns where mining, lumbering or shipping concerns picked up and moved on long, long ago.

Yet, in 1913, the township surrounding Calumet Township bustled with 33,000 souls. Several languages were spoken, due to the large number of European immigrants flocking to the mines, mines that supplied 90 percent of the world's copper in the late 19th and early 20th centuries. Understandably, folks thought the place would only keep growing.

But the mood was turning sour. The July work stoppage was causing headaches and shortages (see previous), but the miners continued to knuckle down because worker pay and job safety were at stake.

The striking miners were led by the charismatic Anna "Big Annie" Clemenc, who wasn't actually a miner herself. She was a volunteer at a church that catered to injured miners. She'd also started the local women's auxiliary of the Western Federation of Miners. The attractive, statuesque, 6-foot 2-inch Annie was quite the figurehead, leading the marches in a gingham dress.

Months went by and the contentious year drew to a close. Annie and the women's auxiliary planned an event to give the children something to take their minds off the grownups' anger and their own hungry bellies. The holiday pageant was to be held on December 24t, on the second floor of the Italian Hall. There would be skits, songs, costumes, and token gifts.

It was a happy time, a time for forgetting, when in the middle of the festivities someone yelled "Fire!" A few headed for the windows, landing in snowbanks. But the majority stampeded the narrow, enclosed staircase that led to the door at the bottom. Tragically, the door opened inward.

Coffins for the Italian Hall dead.

The crush of the others crowding on the staircase created a force that made the door impossible to open.

When it was over, an astounding 73 people — mostly children — were suffocated or trampled to death. Their bodies were laid out on the snow, where families came by to claim the loved ones.

The miner's strike came to an end the next year, in April, after nine long months. The union was broken. Those who were tired of being hungry figured it was a one-man drill or a no-man drill. The strike did achieve an eight-hour work day for the miners, but pay, conditions, and almost everything else stayed the same as before.

It was really the end of an era, though. Calumet was no longer a boomtown. Miners who'd lost their jobs to that one-man drill began leaving shortly after the strike, and with the Great Depression creeping closer, copper prices dropped and the mines began to close down.

The person who yelled "Fire!" at the Italian Hall was never identified, nor was his anti-union motive ever proven, but many settled on that narrative anyway. Woody Guthrie sang about it in the song "1913 Massacre," squarely blaming the companies.

Big Annie Clemenc seems to have fared better than the town. She became a well-known labor organizer and lived another 40 years. She was the first inductee into the Michigan Women's Hall of Fame at 213 West Malcolm X Street in Lansing.

MURDER MAP

Calumet is along highway **M-41**, between Houghton/Hancock and Copper Harbor. Only one archway of the Italian Hall still stands. In the building's place is a small memorial park, on **7th Street**, just south of highway **M-203**.

While there's not a lot of activity in town, and a fair amount of vacant store and home space, these largely stone buildings were built to last. Stroll through the town and you'll see the kind of sandstone, stone and brick construction so characteristic of century-old buildings in the U.P., and you may get a sense that this was once a far more bustling place. There's the ornate Calumet Theatre, said to have hosted some of the big Vaudeville-era names in the early 20th century. The town has refurbished the theater in recent years and hosts events there again.

Of course, the city also sits among the mostly defunct copper mines that made it tick way back when, and to the south are the picturesque twin college towns of Houghton and Hancock perched on the high, steep banks of the Keweenaw Waterway valley.

To the north is Michigan's northernmost community of Copper Harbor, where hikers catch the ferry to Isle Royale National Park. The Keweenaw Peninsula is also one of the most scenic drives in a scenic state.

Although the Upper Peninsula is part of the state of Michigan, there is no land-link between the two. Before the Mackinac Bridge, Michigan travelers to the Upper Peninsula had to take a ferry. Even with nine operating ferries, traffic would back up for 16 miles during deer season.

Getting to the Upper Peninsula

On July 1, 1888, railroad and shipping magnate Cornelius Vanderbilt pronounced at the Grand Hotel's board of directors meeting on Mackinac Island that, "We now have the largest, well-equipped hotel of its kind in the world for a short season business. Now what we need is a bridge across the Straits."

At that point in history, the idea of bridging 3,800 feet was imaginable, but unfeasible. The Brooklyn Bridge, completed in 1883, only had to cross the East River, a mere 1,595.5 feet.

Years and decades went by and various wild ideas were floated around. Someone suggested a tunnel, another had a plan for a series of bridges and causeways starting in Cheboygan.

Michigan Governor Fred Green ordered the State Highway Department in 1923 to set up a ferry service. Five years later, the service was swamped with traffic, and so began more dreams of bridges.

First WWII, then Korea got in the way of labor and materials, but by 1952, private investors from around the country had met the nearly $100 million price tag. At the same time, Michigan legislators passed an act to maintain and operate the structure by taxing gas and license plates. Dr. David B. Steinman designed the 5-mile bridge, and the largest construction fleet ever assembled put the bridge together.

Five construction workers died while building the Mighty Mac. One drowning and one diving accident and three falling accidents. Don't believe the folklore that someone is still encased in the bridge's concrete. They're only trying to give you a chill when you drive over the green behemoth.

Mackinac Bridge, the world's longest suspension bridge between cable anchorages, opened for travel on November 1, 1957. Just in time for deer season.

TWELFTH STREET RIOTS

THE YEAR: 1967
THE CRIME: MURDER
THE MOTIVE: A DIVIDED CITY

WHILE 1967 WAS THE SUMMER OF LOVE IN SAN FRANCISCO, IN DETROIT IT WAS ANYTHING BUT.

There was little love to be found between the increasingly segregated black community and the nearly all-white police force.

The spark that set the fires arrived on a Saturday night at 12th Street and Clairmount, in an area known as Virginia Park — an increasingly poor, black neighborhood. While a few white store owners remained, many had already moved their families out to the suburbs, and most hoped to do the same with their businesses.

Lack of opportunity and the overbearing police presence may have been discussed that July night at the illicit watering hole, or "blind pig." But the real reason for the after-hours gathering was to celebrate the safe return of two friends who'd served in the Vietnam War.

At 3:35 in the morning, after legal clubs had closed their doors for the night, police crashed the party. Everyone was to be arrested. It was well after dawn when officers finished processing all 182 partiers, and the crowd on the street had become more and more irritated. Rumors were circulating that a police officer had beaten a woman while arresting her.

It began with rocks. Glass broke and looters rushed in where windows were missing. The vice squad called for reinforcements. State police, riot squads, and National Guard tanks were sent in at the order of Governor George Romney and President Lyndon Johnson. Five days later, as dozens of buildings lay smoldering in ruins, the death toll stood at 43, mostly black and mostly killed by police.

Devil's Night, Every Night

Detroit and burning buildings have a long history. In fact, the city's motto, "Speramus Meliora; Resurget Cineribus," Latin for "We Hope for Better Things; It Shall Rise From the Ashes," came about because in 1805, nearly the entire city burned to the ground.

Then, there were the race riot fires of the 1967 12th Street Riot.

The 70s saw the beginning of the auto industry exodus and vacant storefronts and homes became targets of what was then called "recreational arson." In 1977, major crime dropped 20% in Detroit, but arson — particularly in Cass Corridor — went up 300%.

Devil's Night (the night before Halloween) arson attacks also became popular at that time, and increased throughout the 80s. On one Devil's Night in 1984, 300 fires were set, winning Detroit an unfortunate Guinness world record. Some people even reserved tables at the revolving restaurant atop the Renaissance Center to watch the city light up with flames and police and fire flashers.

MURDER MAP

After the riots, the epicenter was left in smoldering ruins and the businesses that once dominated **12th** and **Clairmount** have long since been razed. The area is mostly residential now.

Twelfth Street has since been renamed **Rosa Parks Boulevard**, after the civil rights icon. Parks, whose refusal to give up her seat at the front of the bus to a white man in Montgomery, Alabama, helped spark the civil rights movement of the 50s and 60s. Parks moved to Detroit after her activism ended her job and eventually she worked for U.S. Representative John Conyers. Conyers, at one point during the 67 riots, tried to calm things down by climbing on a car and speaking through a bullhorn. When rocks flew his way, he abandoned the idea.

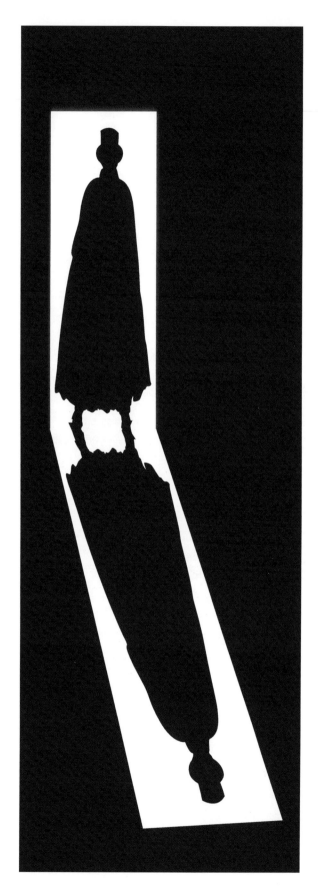

Who's Been Murdering the Motor City?

Detroit started the 20th century with 285,000 people calling it home. It closed out the century with 950,000. Not a bad gain, you might think.

It's what happened in between that's mind-blowing. Detroit became the fastest growing and fastest shrinking major American city of the 20th century. It reached its zenith smack dab in the middle. In 1950 it was the fourth largest metropolis in the United States, with nearly 2 million souls. But census by census the numbers dropped, until they dipped under 1 million. It was a stinging milestone for a city that was a worldwide symbol of American capitalism and ingenuity.

When the century opened, the clanking of steel on steel could be heard around town in small shops. Detroiters made stoves, carriages, and even quite a few cars — or "auto mobiles," motor carriages, runabouts, what have you. When Henry Ford started his ill-fated Detroit Automobile Company in 1899 at 1343 Cass Avenue, his was one of 125 car makers in the city.

By 1900, Detroit's population had already grown one-hundredfold since Stephen Gifford Simmons was hanged (see page 10), but Detroiters hadn't seen anything yet.

Ford's Highland Park Plant, which adopted the assembly line and started rolling out Model Ts for the everyman, was what Henry's great grandchildren might call a game-changer. Other, similar plants opened, and many small car makers consolidated. General Motors was the daddy of all consolidations, bringing together second-tier companies like Buick, Chevrolet and R.E. Olds (Oldsmobile). GM became a behemoth and the richest company in the world for decades. Detroit was the Silicon Valley of the automotive industry.

The booming industry brought lots of jobs. European immigrants, as well as blacks and whites from the South, came in droves. With them came racial and ethnic strife, even as many of them were joining the middle class.

Detroiter Kent Myers drew this series of comics in the late 1980s, after moving to San Fransisco.

kentmyers.com

The Great Depression was hard on the city, with massive layoffs since few people could afford a new car. Yet when World War II came, Detroit soared again as one of the biggest pieces of FDR's Arsenal of Democracy. There was plenty of work here for young women who wanted to be a Rosie the Riveter, as so many young men were serving overseas. Warplanes and tanks rode down local assembly lines instead of family sedans.

When the war ended, the city's population was still rising. Why would anyone think it wouldn't continue?

Yet the second half of the century was not so kind to the Motor City. The town that revolutionized transportation also built freeways that — along with crime and racial tension — encouraged white flight. The suburbs grew while the city began to sputter. The 1967 race riots inspired more white people to head for the hills — Farmington Hills, Bloomfield Hills, the greener pastures of the suburbs.

Meanwhile, some thriving neighborhoods, like Black Bottom and Poletown, were bulldozed to make way for freeway cloverleafs and more auto plants. In the 1970s, poverty and crime skyrocketed and Detroit snidely became known as Murder City. Motown Records left for Los Angeles, abandoning Detroit and the sound the two had made together. Devil's Night, October 30th, became an annual orgy of arson. Japanese car makers continued to cut into the U.S. auto market and layoffs kept coming.

By the end of the century, Detroit had been largely left for dead in the eyes of the world.

Now, a few years after the city's bankruptcy, certain neighborhoods are filling in and getting fixed up. Still, large, littered swaths speak of a huge, industrial ghost town.

Detroit is definitely not dead, though a whole lot of suspects have plunged their daggers into its heart.

LONG LINGER THE KING

THE YEAR: 1812
THE CRIME: MURDER
THE MOTIVE: SELF CORONATION

JAMES JESSE STRANG HAD A ROYAL FIXATION.

When he was a kid, he dreamed of finding a way to marry Queen Victoria, the young monarch of England. He also set about to "rival Caesar or Napoleon" in accomplishments. Although he never managed to add Victoria to his string of wives, he did become king. And like Napoleon, he crowned himself.

Strang's rise to royalty began in 1844, when he joined the Church of the Latter Day Saints. The Church was in hard times, though, splitting apart over dogma and the crushing weight of anti-Mormonism. One of the last things founder Joseph Smith did was send young Strand to Wisconsin to establish a mission. Soon after that, Smith was murdered.

Smith's death created a power struggle, and Strang did his best to convince followers that he was the one best suited to shepherd the flock. He didn't sway the majority — the largest group famously departed for Utah — but he did have some 12,000 supporters. Strang led a handful of them northward, to Beaver Island.

At that time, the 55-square-mile island, the largest in Lake Michigan, was populated mostly by Irish immigrants. He and his congregation soon came to dominate the population, and that fact must have produced Strang's eureka moment: small island plus dozens of devoted followers equals resurrection of the kinghood fantasy.

Strang declared himself, in 1850, King of the Kingdom of God on Beaver Island.

A monarchy is not a democracy, and Strang's new authority gave him unlimited power to change the rules. Originally opposed to polygamy, he legalized the practice, eventually accumulating a brood of five wives and 14 children. He devised a dress code for women consisting of loose-fitting clothes — bloomers at all times — and had husbands whipped if their wives didn't comply. He banned liquor and levied taxes.

132

BEAVER ISLAND LIMITED, BEAVER ISLAND, MICH.

PUBLISHED FOR ADA M. WILKINSON

Why did Strang go to Beaver Island? The answer is cordwood. Cordwood — the de-barked ends of logs — was the main source of fuel aboard the main source of transportation —steamers — on the Great Lakes. In 1847, James Strang showed up on Beaver Island with a couple of friends and spent some time chopping wood. When he needed a kingdom, and an economy to support it, Beaver Island was at the top of his mind.

Needless to say, he made some enemies. First there were the former residents, who got sick of being ordered around by a king with a crown made of tin, bedazzled with glass stars. And then, there were the whippings if one's wife wore the wrong thing. Many former supporters left the island, spreading tales. President Millard Fillmore even got involved, ordering an investigation of King Strang and his practices.

But a trial in Detroit and a successful defense only helped get him elected to the state legislature in 1853. Two years later, he won the seat again. He made sure the island sustained itself as a cordwood fueling dock for the shipping industry, helped organize large parts of the state into counties and townships and fought to clamp down on the practice of trading liquor to Native Americans. Many islanders hated him already for taking it over, and that last issue won him enemies all the way to the Straits.

Some in his flock began to hate him, too, particularly for those whippings. But just days before his murder, Strang was standing firm: "We laugh with bitter scorn at all these threats," he wrote in his newspaper the *Northern Islander*, the first of its kind in northern Michigan.

On Monday, June 16, 1856, only a year into his second term as state rep, a disgruntled whippee invited Strang to the dock for a meeting regarding the king's impossible orders. Two other men sneaked up behind him and shot him point-blank in the head and upper back. As he lay on the ground, he was shot once more in the cheek for good measure.

Strang was stubborn. He held on for 12 days, warning his followers that the enemy was coming. And so it was. Less than a month later, the remaining Strangites (about 2,600) were forcibly sent packing — most without their luggage or their money — and life returned to the way it was before the island community became a kingdom.

MURDER MAP

Beaver Island is accessible by ferry from Charlevoix, and is popular with tourists. It's part of a string of islands that extend southwest into the northern part of the lake from the Straits of Mackinac. It has a large Irish population, and is sometimes called America's Emerald Isle. The island now has two airports and 550 residents.

The island is known for its bars and restaurants, biking and hiking trails, quiet beaches and inland lakes for fishing. It's primarily for vacationers who want to slow down the pace and don't mind the stores closing earlier than on the mainland.

Strand's good name wasn't entirely wiped out by his bad end. His survey of the island's natural history, published by the Smithsonian, remained the definitive work on that subject for almost 100 years.

After Joseph Smith's murder, Strang alleged that an angel had ordained him the successor. Lacking human support, he also produced a Letter of Appointment, signed by Smith nine days before his death. About 12,000 members of the Latter Day Saints accepted his claim. Some maintain, however, that the signature is a forgery.

A KILLER HANDSHAKE

THE YEAR: 1901
THE CRIME: MURDER
THE MOTIVE: TERRORISM

LEE HARVEY OSWALD AND JOHN WILKES BOOTH ARE DARKLY FAMOUS NAMES IN AMERICAN LORE.

Of course, they killed presidents John F. Kennedy and Abraham Lincoln.

Mentioning the name of Leon Czolgosz, though, is likely to be met with a blank stare. Czolgosz murdered William McKinley, one of two other presidents to die from an assassin's bullet. Both McKinley and the other victim, James Garfield, were from Ohio, which might have been part of the motive. Just kidding, but take that, Buckeyes!

Leon, an avowed anarchist and socialist, was born in Detroit of Polish immigrant parents and worked in a steel mill as a child, before the push for child-labor laws. He is believed to have spent part of his boyhood in Alpena, though his family moved around a lot. As an adult, he lived in Cleveland, Ohio, working at a factory. He lost his job in 1893, as the country was tumbling into a depression. When he wasn't working odd jobs, he was reading about and talking to socialists and anarchists — the latter part of a growing movement around the globe opposed to any authority.

McKinley was elected in 1896 and presided over an improving economy and victory in the Spanish-American War. He was riding high in September, 1901, just a few months into his second term, as he greeted the public at the Pan-American Exhibition in Buffalo, New York.

Czolgosz, meanwhile, had not prospered along with the rest of the country. With his wallet and his belly empty most of the time, anarchistic fervor filled his head more and more. He'd seen a spate of anarchist assassinations or attempts in Europe. And now, the American President (who he saw as inherently corrupt because he was part of the government, any government) was going to be relatively nearby. On September 6, 1901, Czolgosz went to Buffalo, dressed in his finest and stood in line in the Temple of Music pavilion to shake hands with McKinley.

Artist's rendition of McKinley assassination.

Czolgosz in jail.

In his hand was a .32 caliber revolver hidden under a handkerchief. As McKinley reached out to shake, Czolgosz fired two shots. McKinley died several days later of gangrene from the wound and Vice President Theodore Roosevelt was sworn in as the new leader.

Justice was swift.

Czolgosz was tried, convicted and given a high-voltage ride in the electric chair less than two months from when he fired the shots into McKinley's gut. His last words were: "I killed the president because he was the enemy of the good people — the working people."

It's pretty hard to imagine, in this day of clamped down security, someone being allowed to shake the President's hand while concealing a gun under a hanky. So where was the Secret Service in all this?

Looking for counterfeiters.

That's right. The Secret Service was invented to keep counterfeit money from destroying the economy. In Civil War days, one-third of the paper money going through the hands of soldiers, storekeepers and everyone else was fake. And they didn't even have photocopiers back then!

Ironically, Lincoln signed the agency into existence earlier on the day his assassin walked into his theater balcony and shot him in the head. Yet it took two more presidential assassinations before the Secret Service expanded into the President-protecting business.

McKinley's death was what did it. Of course they were there when Kennedy was shot, but were no match for sniper fire and a president in an open convertible. They fared better during attempts on the lives of Gerald Ford and Ronald Reagan.

THE TALKING SKULL

THE YEAR: 1907
THE CRIME: MURDER
THE MOTIVE: ONLY THE BONES KNOW

SISTER MARY JANINA CAME TO THE GENTLE HILLS AND ORCHARDS OF ISADORE, A SETTLEMENT NORTH OF CEDAR, TO TEACH THE 200 OR SO CHILDREN OF FARMING FAMILIES FROM EASTERN EUROPE.

One August day in 1907, after she'd been there about a year, the parish priest left for an afternoon of fishing on Lake Leelanau with some friends. Sister Janina waved and closed her shade on the hot sun. Two other nuns and the housekeeper also stayed behind.

When Father Andrew Bieniawski and company returned with their catch that evening, Sister Janina was nowhere to be found. Her rosary hung from a doorknob and her Bible lay open on a windowsill. Priest, fellow sisters and neighbors called out to the churchyard and nearby farms, but nobody answered.

That night, Father Andrew led a frantic search of the grounds and outbuildings by lantern. Again, Sister Mary Janina was nowhere to be found.

Days, weeks, years went by and nothing turned up in Isadore or the woods or lowlands of Leelanau County that hinted at her fate. Was it foul play or did the sister who grew up an orphan get tired of the religious life and sneak away?

Leads were chased down to their dead-ends. Neighbors reported a woman's voice singing from swamps out beyond their fields. Father Andrew was reassigned to a church in Manistee.

Then, 11 years later, as a new priest was planning to tear down the old wooden church and rebuild it in brick, he received a warning. Priests from nearby parishes whispered that a remodel would bring about a scandal to rock his unassuming little church.

The cryptic forecasts worried the minister. He and the sexton scoured the area for clues to what secrets might be lurking in the old church. Then, in the dirt floor of the basement, they discovered what appeared to be a shallow grave. They brushed away the dirt and, you guessed it, found bones. Bits of a nun's brown habit were wrapped around the skeleton and the skull was smashed in. It was surely Sister Mary Janina.

They quietly re-buried the remains in the church cemetery, unmarked, and dusted themselves off. That was that, they hoped. Scandal averted.

New unmarked graves in the churchyard, however, don't go unnoticed for long in a close-knit community.

Sheriff John Kinnucan, sensing some movement in a bothersome old mystery, caught wind of it. Before long, Sister Mary Janina was being unearthed once again, and the sheriff was talking to the nuns, priest and housekeeper who lived there when she waved goodbye forever.

Rumors about unholy liaisons between Father Andrew and Sister Mary Janina swirled anew around the hills. Some have speculated a botched abortion was the cause of death, and that the skull was smashed by accident after she died.

There was also Stanislawa or Stella, the Polish housekeeper. She was often heard bullying and belittling the timid nun in her broken English. The sheriff chose her as his prime suspect and arrested her. His supposed interrogation methods were macabre, straight out of a nightmare. In a candle-lit room, he manipulated a human skull to make its jaw move. "You killed me," the skull spoke over and over again to the horrified suspect. The woman who provided the voice for the enhanced interrogation method later testified that she heard Stella confess to the murder.

Whether or not she actually confessed was, and is, a matter of debate. It's believed that she bitterly resented a romantic affair between Father Andrew and Sister Mary Janina, but she denied both the murder and the confession. The jury convicted her nevertheless, and she was sentenced to life in prison.

Sister Mary Janina's bones, by the way, also made an appearance in the trial. Lawyers arranged them on a table and argued over them. Then, just like Sister Mary Janina did on that hot afternoon in 1907 when she still had flesh, her remains slipped away to nobody knows where.

Postcard from showing housekeeper Stella Lipczynska inside the Leelanau County Jail, Leland, MI. Collection of Dave Tinder.

MURDER MAP

Holy Rosary Church is located at **6982 South Schomberg Road**, north of the village of Cedar, known for its Polish roots and an annual summer Polka Festival. The brick church building that was being planned when Sister Janina's bones were found, still stands.

PIGS EAT ANYTHING

THE YEAR: 1985
THE CRIME: MURDER
THE MOTIVE: WE DON'T LIKE YOU

FIREARM DEER HUNTING SEASON IN MICHIGAN
RUNS THE LAST HALF OF NOVEMBER.

As the leaves ferment on the floor of the woods, hundreds of
thousands of hunters head to points north. Detroiters, Ohioans
and Chicagoans fill up the forests, the rustic rental cabins, the
Indian casinos and the bars. Hundreds of mom-and-pop shops
love to see them coming.

Brian Ognjan and David Tyll were just two more drops in
the sea of camouflage and neon orange. The two friends from
northside Detroit suburbs ended their hunting day at a bar in
Mio. As the night wore on, they drank more, and more, and
became increasingly obnoxious. Lewd language with some of
the women wasn't exactly making new friends.

Unfortunately, the local Duvall brothers took a pretty intense
dislike to them. Raymond "JR" and Donald "Coco" Duvall
were well known in the area, and most people tried to stay
on their good sides. There was a queasy feeling in the air that
between the Duvalls and the suburbanites, things could get
ugly. They did. When those two 20-something down-staters
walked out the tavern door, they disappeared without a trace.

Not only were they gone, but the Ford Bronco they drove up
I-75 to get there had also disappeared.

To the world outside Mio, a town of 2,000 inhabitants east
of Grayling, it was a mystery. The police knew there was
something rotten, and it was no secret that the missing guys
had exchanged unpleasantries with the Duvalls. Still, without
physical evidence — no bodies, no car, no nothing— they
might as well have been abducted by aliens. Nobody would
talk, either, for fear of the Duvalls' wrath.

For nearly two decades, police tried to piece together a case
against the brothers. A woman named Barbara Boudro was
also losing sleep over the secret she knew but didn't dare tell.

You see, on the night the hunters disappeared, Barbara saw the Duvalls and their victims outside of her house. Out in a neighboring field, in front of the lit headlights of a truck, the Duvalls made a party out of a beating. Fists, boots and a baseball bat were applied as the men pleaded for their lives. The brothers howled with laughter when one of the victims wet his pants, then they beat him some more.

Barbara and a friend tried to lay low. The last thing they wanted was for the Duvalls to know what they had seen.

But the brothers had seen. Then came a knock on the door.

"You saw nothing, you heard nothing. Pigs need to eat too," one of the brothers yelled through the closed door.

Finally, 18 years after the horrible night, police pieced together a case, but they needed Barbara's testimony. They knew she was holding back. They didn't blame her, but enough was enough. She bravely and belatedly unloaded her gruesome secret, and prosecutors put the Duvall brothers away for life.

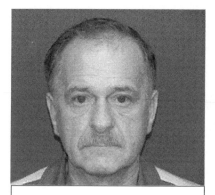

RAYMOND WILBUR DUVALL JR

MDOC Number: 476519

Racial Identification: White

Gender: Male

Hair: Brown

Eyes: Blue

Height: 5Ð 9Ð

Weight: 160 lbs.

Date of Birth: 11/21/1950 (61)

Current Status: Prisoner

Earliest Release Date: LIFE

Assigned Location: Newberry Correctional Facility

Security Level: II

Date of Offense: 11/23/1985

County: Oscoda

Date of Sentence: 11/13/2003

Conviction Type: Jury

ALIASES MARKS, SCARS & TATTOOS

Scar- Lower Left Ankle

Scar- Lower Right Ankle

Tattoo- Center Genitalia

Tattoo- Lower Left Arm – Hearts

Tattoo- Upper Left Arm – Rose

DONALD DEAN DUVALL

MDOC Number: 476526

Racial Identification: White

Gender: Male

Hair: Black

Eyes: Hazel

Height: 5Ð 5Ð

Weight: 150 lbs.

Date of Birth: 02/26/1952 (60)

Current Status: Prisoner

Earliest Release Date: LIFE

Assigned Location: Chippewa Correctional Facility

Security Level: II

Date of Offense: 11/23/1985

County: Oscoda

Date of Sentence: 11/13/2003

Conviction Type: Jury

ALIASES MARKS, SCARS & TATTOOS

Tattoo- Center Left Arm – D.D., Eagle

Tattoo- Center Right Shoulder – Cherry

Tattoo- Center Right Wrist – Coke

Tattoo- Left Wrist – DD

MURDER MAP

Mio is situated in the valley of the Au Sable River, a stream revered for its trout fishing. The town is along **M-72**, between Grayling and Lake Huron.

AN UNCLE IN THE FURNITURE BIZ

THE YEAR: 1974
THE CRIME: MURDER
THE MOTIVE: DANGEROUS LIAISONS

"YOU'VE GOT AN UNCLE IN THE FURNITURE BUSINESS, JOSHUA DOORE, JOSHUA DOORE…."

In the early 1970s, that jingle hit the airwaves in metro Detroit and instantly stuck in people's brains. It was for a new furniture store chain that cut prices by cutting out the delivery. Or, as the jingle says:

". . . You pick it out in the showroom, pick it up at the warehouse,

And take it home in the crate! Yeah!

You've got an uncle in the furniture business. . . ."

In the TV commercial, the actor sang the jingle in a recliner with an ever-increasing chorus line around him. He and his recliner were taking a ride on a forklift destined for the trunk of a car.

So the gallows humor was flowing strong when Harvey Leon Leach showed up dead in the trunk of his own car in a Southfield parking lot. Most people had never heard of Leach, but it turned out he was the 34-year-old chairman of Joshua Doore Furniture Company and everyone had heard of that.

Leach bought the struggling Robinson Furniture chain in 1971, renamed it, brought in a more stylish line and appeared to be saving the business. So far, so good. He was young, he was a millionaire and he was falling in with the wrong crowd.

For some reason, instead of heading to a bank like most businesses, he took out an expansion loan from Detroit mob boss Anthony "Tony Jack" Giacalone. Now Tony Jack wanted to be a larger part of the business. Leach was unhappy and the chain's finances were suffering.

On March 16, 1974, the two parties were supposed to get together and work out a deal where a Giacalone proxy would buy the business from a disgruntled Leach. Dangerous liaisons.

Ah, but there was also a woman. Rather two.

Leach was getting married in a few days to Beverly Adelson, but he was also carrying on with Tony Jack's little brother's girlfriend while the little brother was away in the pen. Neither woman got Leach. His body was found in a car trunk, beaten, his throat slit, just an hour before the scheduled wedding.

The murder is still unsolved, and it includes some of the main suspects in the Jimmy Hoffa disappearance (see page 143). Tony Jack Giacalone was a suspect, as was brother Billy Jack. The suspected trigger man was Leonard Schultz, a friend of Leach and the mob associate who set up the first loan. He was also the Giacalone's #1 Teamster troubleshooter. Harvey Leach had been scheduled to meet with Schultz on the morning of his disappearance, so he was long thought to be the one witness who could help solve the murder. Schultz died of natural causes in 2013 at the age of 96. He never uttered a word.

Detroit Free Press, August 8, 1976

MURDER MAP

There's not a lot to distinguish the intersection of **13 Mile** and **Southfield Road** from a lot of other busy, commercial intersections northwest of Detroit. That may be why it was a good place to drop off a body.

Resurrection

After Leach's death, the Joshua Doore Furniture Company went into bankruptcy. It was purchased by a Giacalone associate and brought back to life under the old name of Robinson Furniture. In and out of business over the years, it returned in 2010 under new ownership.

NO BODY, LITTLE DOUBT

THE YEAR: 1975
THE CRIME: MURDER
THE MOTIVE: ETERNAL TEAMSTER TIME-OUT

JIMMY HOFFA, THE FAMOUS UNION LEADER WITH WELL-KNOWN MOB TIES, DIDN'T ACTUALLY HAVE HIS LAST MEAL ON JULY 30, 1975, IN THE MACHUS RED FOX RESTAURANT ON TELEGRAPH ROAD.

He was waiting in his car for some dining companions — Detroit mobster Anthony "Tony Jack" Giacalone and New Jersey mobster Anthony "Tony Pro" Provenzano — to show up first. And then Hoffa disappeared, starting a mystery that has only intensified over the last 40 years.

Hoffa had been the president of the Teamsters union, with some 1.5 million members, from 1958 to 1971. The Teamsters started in the Midwest, organizing truck drivers and warehouse workers. Exceptionally adept at tactics like "quickie strikes," he managed to leverage union strength, increase membership, win contracts and take the Teamsters national.

The problem was that many truck drivers were controlled, and often owned, by the mob.

Attorney General Robert F. Kennedy tried several times to put Hoffa away for corruption, and under Kennedy's "Get Hoffa" initiative, the labor leader was finally convicted of bribing a juror in 1964. He was sentenced to eight years, then another five for fraud. He served five and was pardoned by President Richard Nixon. But the condition was a time-out from union activity for nine years, or until 1980. Hoffa was trying to break that ban when he disappeared.

Hoffa arrived at the Machus Red Fox for his lunch meeting around 2 in the afternoon, and waited in his 1974 Pontiac Grandville for his associates to show. He was last heard from at 2:45 p.m. when he called home to say he was still waiting. The family reported him missing the next day.

Speculation, jokes and morbid curiosity have surrounded the case since the very beginning. There have been rumors

that his body was buried under the Meadowlands football stadium in New Jersey. A driveway was dug up in Roseville. Zilch. Even now, the FBI gets a tip every so often and plows up a field somewhere. Like the summer of 2013 when Tony Zerilli — whose family name had been a fixture in the Detroit underworld since the 1920s — told police that Hoffa was buried near the Oakland County town of Milford, about 20 miles west of the Machus Red Fox. Hoffa was declared officially dead in 1982. So far, none of the tips or hunches have uncovered his bones.

MURDER MAP

Hoffa's 45-minute-or-so wait in the parking lot is what made the Machus Red Fox a legend.

The restaurant building is still there at **6676 Telegraph Road**, about four miles north of I-696 in the tony Bloomfield Township. New owners call the Italian restaurant Andiamo.

A Pair of Jacks?
• • • • • • • • • • • • • • •

The Giacalone's fingerprints were all over the murder of Harvey Leach and disappearance of Jimmy Hoffa. But there's one huge difference: Leach was left somewhere he would undoubtedly be found. Hoffa, however, was disappeared.

It would seem to this writer, with no credentials other than being a fan of "The Sopranos," that the difference is one of respect.

Hoffa had played with the big boys for years, while Leach was a recent business success whose name the public didn't recognize until he died. Plus, Leach may have overreached, both financially and sexually. He was, therefore, put out like the trash.

RAISING HELL

THE YEAR: 1990
THE CRIME: MURDER
THE MOTIVE: KICKS

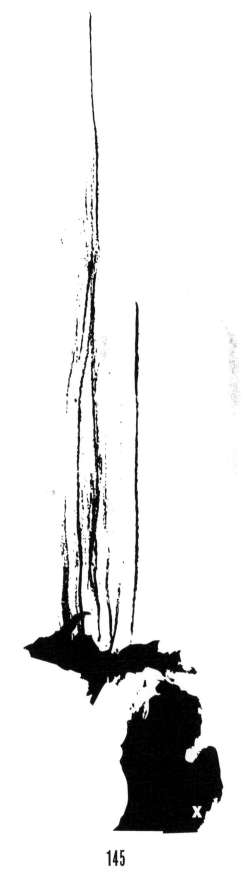

IT WAS A TYPICAL EVENING IN THE PENA HOME IN WARREN.

Known as a house with noisy parties, a hang-out for neighborhood kids, Augustin Pena was doing just that with his cousin Jaime "Jimbo" Rodriguez, Jr.

Rodriguez, 21, thought of himself as a tattoo artist and satanist — he had a pentagram and a goat's head tattooed on his chest. He'd been living at the Pena house for a couple of years, since his mother committed suicide. And he was doing a little scratching work that night. Kids were coming and going. The usual.

Fifteen-year-old Stephanie Dubay showed up. She'd just argued with her parents and wasn't going back. The party got loud enough that someone called the cops. Later, someone else offered Stephanie a ride home. She didn't take it.

The next morning, the house was quiet. Pena's mom was out and Stephanie, who'd slept over, was still asleep.

Rodriguez and Pena were sitting at the kitchen table.

Jimbo turned to his cousin and said, "Let's kill Steph."

"You serious?"

"Yeah."

It was that matter-of-fact, as Rodriguez later told reporters. He also said that Stephanie was a pest, always wanting to hang out with the guys. He didn't like her.

So, the two went to work, laying down newspapers on the basement floor, as if they were carving a pumpkin.

Pena, who was Stephanie's age, went upstairs and woke the girl up. He led her downstairs, then held her by the neck as Rodriguez stabbed her 10 times in the chest and back with a kitchen knife.

They looked at the bloody corpse on the newspapers, and then came to the same sick conclusion. They started to take the body apart.

"We just read each other's minds and went for it," was Rodriguez's nonchalant explanation. He considered keeping a finger as a charm to wear around his neck.

They filled five garbage bags with body parts, buried four in the yard, and stuck one in the car in the garage. But the head, they skinned and put in a plastic bag in the freezer. Apparently, they planned to keep it as a "memento or a conversation piece."

Typical, again, of a party house, guests began to arrive. Rodriguez bragged about the head in his freezer, and two women went to look. Horrified, they left the house with the hideously souvenir and went directly to the police.

Pena was tried as an adult, and juries found them both guilty. They were both sentenced to life in prison. It's hard to imagine a colder murder than this one.

DAYMON J. HARTLEY/Detroit Free Press

Police and technicians remove evidence Thursday from the Warren house where, police believe, a teenage girl was killed. They said the victim may have been a 15-year-old Clinton Township girl.

Detroit Free Press, July 13, 1990

MURDER MAP

The home where Stephanie was murdered was on **Jean Road**, near **11 Mile** and **Hoover** roads. **Jean** is a long suburban subdivision street with mid-20th century brick ranch homes, mature shade trees between the sidewalks and curbs.

The northside suburb of Warren is Michigan's third largest city after Detroit and Grand Rapids. It's home to the massive General Motors Tech Center.

Stephanie was buried in Clinton Grove Cemetery of Macomb County, in Clinton Township near the home from which she'd run away.

BORDER BETWEEN LIFE AND DEATH

THE YEAR: 1883
THE CRIME: MURDER
THE MOTIVE: NO LOVE

THIS CASE HAS IT ALL: A LOVE TRIANGLE, AN INTERNATIONAL TRIAL, A JAIL ESCAPE AND A PROLONGED EXECUTION.

Luke Phipps was a hard-luck immigrant from Oxfordshire, England. His wife, Effie, was a postmaster's daughter from upstate New York. Together, they'd been drifting around the East, looking for work, squabbling and adding infant mouths to the Phipps clan.

They found their way to the bustling Great Lakes port of Detroit, which had grown from the size of L'Anse to twice the size of Lansing (both current figures) in just 50 years. That's where Luke found a job managing a billiard hall. They rented a flat and settled in, but there it all went wrong. Three children turned into four, and in an effort to save money, Luke rented a room to the man who would steal Effie's heart. The man was his co-worker at the billiard hall — Harry Livingstone.

It wasn't long before Luke noticed Effie and their tenant talking a bit too much and standing a little too close. Suspicion turned to jealousy which erupted in violence. On Christmas morning, 1882, Luke took his fists to Effie. The police arrived and broke it up. Luke was arrested and spent the first month of 1883 looking through bars.

When released, he walked home to find an empty house — his wife, the children and Harry Livingstone had cleared out without a trace. In fact, Effie had taken the kids to live at the Home for the Friendless — yes, that's really what they called it — while she and her lover Livingstone nested together under assumed names.

Despite her dubious maternal instincts, Effie was serious about starting a new life. She'd filed for divorce and was doing what she could to block Luke from seeing the children. Luke fought back, and at one point, Effie was arrested for adultery. Yeah, getting arrested for adultery was a thing then, too.

Several months of ugly break-up ensued before Effie gave up and moved the family across the river to Windsor, Canada.

Luke had kept his eyes and ears open, though, and on August 19, when news came of Effie landing in Detroit for a visit, he picked up his gun. He didn't catch up with her until she was boarding the ferry for the return trip to Windsor. Luke slunk on board and laid low as the ferry rumbled at the dock. Once the boat pushed off toward Canada, pool hall Luke got up and marched decisively toward his target. Effie was no fool. She saw him coming and yelled, but yelling rarely stops a bullet, and three pistol shots brought her down. When the ferry sidled in on the Canadian side, Effie lay dead on the deck.

Luke was thrown in a Canadian jail, but lawyers were now involved and things got sticky. Before his trial, Luke's attorney argued that the crime had been committed before the boat reached the international border. He killed her in Michigan, in other words. That was an important legal point, since Michigan had outlawed the death penalty almost 40 years earlier (see page 10). Ontario, on the other hand, was still giving its gallows a pretty decent workout.

Luke's attorney lost that point and the trial went ahead in Canada, resulting in a date with the noose for Luke Phipps.

He was locked in Sandwich Gaol to await his doom. He wasn't going to take it lying down. He and two other murderers managed to break out of their cell by — cliché of clichés — filing the bars.

Phipps and his co-escapees sneaked back into the United States, and Luke actually made it as far as Pullman, Illinois, a booming new company town and suburb of Chicago named after the railroad magnate. He even found work at a hotel, but his luck ran out when the son of a sheriff recognized him. The world was a smaller place back then.

On June 17, 1884, Luke was hanged in Windsor. When he stopped twitching, the authorities took him down from the scaffold and tried to resuscitate him to determine that he was, in fact, dead. Nope. Luke breathed again, but not for long. Windsor got a two-for-one when Luke expired under the watchful eyes of his jailers.

S.S. Landsdowne to Windsor in 1905.

MURDER MAP

Luke Phipps was employed at J&B Armstrong's billiard hall, in a section where **Jefferson Avenue** meets **Woodward**. In those days, it was an area bustling with horse-drawn trolleys and pedestrians. Nowadays, it would be somewhere between the City County Building (with its Spirit of Detroit statue) and Cobo Hall.

Luke Phipps hopped on the ferry off a dock that was at the foot of **Woodward**. **Woodward** now ends at **Jefferson**, across from Hart Plaza and the Joe Louis fist sculpture. The preferred passage to Windsor from the downtown area these days is the Detroit-Windsor Tunnel, completed in 1930.

In a cruel twist for poor Effie Phipps, she must spend eternity next to the man who killed her. Luke's body was laid to rest next to hers in the sprawling Woodmere Cemetery at **9400 West Fort Street**. They are among 200,000 souls buried there, or about the population of Grand Rapids. If you're planning a visit, you may walk over the notorious couple in Section A, Lot 840, grave numbers 13 and 14 without even knowing it. Their graves were never marked. Some say it's because of poverty, while others claim it was out of fear that people would vandalize their markers.

The Home for the Friendless was operated by Presbyterian women at **72 Brush Street**, between **Larned** and **Congress** streets. The area where this would have been is now occupied by tall buildings throwing shade on a few old surviving bars and restaurants, including the favorite Irish watering hole, the Old Shillelagh.

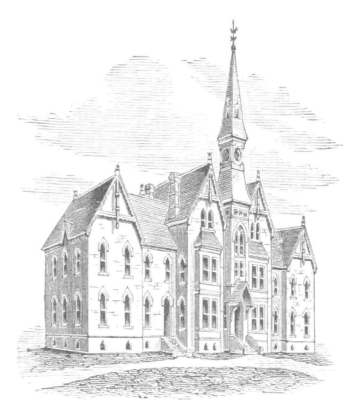

THE HOME OF THE FRIENDLESS.

Woodmere Cemetery
• •

The Phipps have famous neighbors in Woodmere Cemetery, including Henry Leland, who founded the Lincoln and Cadillac car companies, and David Buick, who started the auto brand bearing his name and died broke. Namesakes of Carhartt work clothes, Vernors pop (don't call it soda in Michigan) and Scripps-Howard newspapers are also beneath the cemetery's sod.

One of the more notorious figures resting in Woodmere is Private Eddie Slovik, who died by firing squad during World War II. A poor Polish kid from Detroit, he became the only United States soldier executed for desertion since the Civil War. Frank Sinatra heard the story, and in 1960 announced his plan to produce a movie entitled "The Execution of Private Slovik." He chose blacklisted Hollywood screenwriter Albert Maltz to write the script, for which Sinatra was quickly accused of Communist sympathies. At the time, Sinatra was also lending his voice to John F. Kennedy's presidential campaign. Kennedy advisers saw nothing but trouble, and persuaded Sinatra to scrap the project. In 1974, Martin Sheen played Slovik in a TV movie of the same name.

THE LAST WORD

THE YEAR: 1995
THE CRIME: MURDER
THE MOTIVE: A MAN SCORNED

ON A HOT AUGUST NIGHT IN 1995, APPROACHING MIDNIGHT, DELETHA WORD WAS HANGING OUT ON BELLE ISLE WITH HER DOG.

She'd been chatting with friends and smoking a little reefer laced with angel dust, or PCP.

When her dog scampered under a car, she crouched down to get it and put her hand on a passing Chevy Monte Carlo as a signal to stop.

Unfortunately, it happened to be Martell Welch Jr.'s car. All 300 pounds, 6-foot 4-inches of him got out and approached Deletha, a slight 4-foot 11. Her small dog bounded out from under the car. She took the dog into the roadway and began dancing with friends. Martell Welch and friends taunted Deletha Word and yelled at passing cars:

"Hit that bitch, roll over that bitch."

Friends recall that Welch, 19, was also crudely hitting on Word, who was 33 and had a daughter. He was grabbing at her and not taking no for an answer. Finally, she just had to get out of there.

She was so upset as she ran for her car that she left her dog behind.

But she probably didn't notice, as Martell and his friends had run after her in hot pursuit. In the heat and jumble of distractions, her car scraped against his Monte Carlo. She kept going. She turned onto the bridge to get away from the island and Welch.

The Belle Isle Bridge is a half-mile with two lanes of traffic running each way. On a normal day, the crossing can take less than a minute. Not on hot summer nights. And back in the 1990s, the island park had an unruly reputation for cruising and partying throughout the night.

Sure enough, up ahead the traffic was slowing and Martell's Chevy was growing larger in her rear-view mirror. When he pulled in right behind her, Deletha panicked and threw her car into reverse, crunching Martell's front bumper.

Four men burst out of the car, and Martell ran up to Deletha's window, yanking her half out of the driver seat. Screaming in her face, he smashed her head over and over with his fist. Somehow, he then got her out of the car, dragging her by the hair, and smashed her face into the hood of her car, over and over.

Traffic continued to congeal on the bridge as people stepped out of their cars, horrified. As Welch tore off her clothes, smacked her, and even lifted her off her feet to swing her around, not one of the 40 to 100 witnesses offered the victim any help. (One man said he called 911, but as you will see, it did no good.)

Again Martell yelled at the crowd: "Anybody want some of this bitch? Because she has to pay for my car."

Welch, a high school football player who'd recently lost a chance to try out at Ferris State because of bad grades, then threw Deletha down on the pavement, kicked her in the head and went to grab a tire iron from his trunk. He began to use it on her car, his friends helping. In those blurred, hellish moments, Deletha Word had taken more blows, humiliation and cruelty than most anyone could endure, and she may have thought the tire iron was coming for her next. And whatever the drugs she had used, her choices were crystal clear. She climbed onto the bridge railing. Catching sight of her, Martell raged, "You can't go out that way," and came toward her. Deletha let go. The crowd gasped.

A couple of late shifters, just getting off work, saw a woman go over the bridge. They pulled over and ran down the embankment. But as they swam toward her, she seemed to be frantically trying to escape them. She may have mistaken one of them for her tormentor.

Deletha's body washed up downriver a couple of days later. She had drowned, and one of her legs had been chopped off by a boat propeller. She left behind her thirteen-year-old daughter.

Martell and his friends drove away from the scene of the crime and were only arrested the next day when police spotted a car matching witness descriptions. Martell was sentenced to 16–40 years for second-degree murder.

Your Town
• • • • • • • • •

The AAA Foundation for Traffic Safety estimates that over 1,200 incidents of road rage are reported every year in the U.S. Boston, Miami, Los Angeles, New York and Phoenix are considered capitals of the worst offenders.

MURDER MAP

The island park Belle Isle is widely considered one of the gems of Detroit. Still owned by the city, it has been managed as a Michigan state park since 2013. Belle Isle is home to an aquarium, a nature zoo and the Detroit Yacht Club. A system of greenhouses and winding roads, plus a half-mile beach make it a popular spot for people to gather.

ACKNOWLEDGMENTS

Thank you so much to the professionals at Mission Point Press, particularly Heather Lee Shaw, whose design and editing goes straight to the heart of the subject matter. I truly could not have done it without you!

Thank you to my good friend Anne Stanton, for your integrity and imagination and to you both for introducing me to Doug Weaver and his immense knowledge of publishing. Thank you for all you do for writers.

Thank you to Leigh Wietsma for helping spread the word about this book.

Thank you to Gail Roberts, Mary Fraquelli and the rest at Kingsley Branch Library (and the Traverse Area District Library of which they are a part), who let me take my overdues to the absolute limit, and who combed all the nooks and crannies of the Michigan inter-library loan system for me.

Thank you to Dan Carr for helping me find some of the locations listed here.

Thank you to Maria and the boys for putting up with me talking about murder for an entire Michigan winter.

Thank you to Gail Hershenzon, of Woodmere Cemetery, for your historical knowledge of Woodmere and beyond.

Thank you to the Library of Michigan in Lansing for your extensive collection of newspapers on microfilm. It's so much easier now that I can email myself dozens of pages in an afternoon. Thank you also, to the many fine newspapers in Michigan, admirably chronicling the lives of the state and your communities for generations.

Thank you to the crime web sites that help me put pieces of many stories together.

Thank you to Cathy Dennis of Bath Middle School; and for that school's in-school museum and tribute to the 39 children who lost their lives so long ago to a mad man.

Thank you to the talented Coreene Kreiser of Tavla Studio for the author photo.

And thank you to the many fine authors who have researched and written about individual cases or collections of cases before me.

ABOUT THE AUTHOR

Tavla Studio

Tom Carr is an independent writer and journalist in Northern Michigan who spent 25 years in daily newspapers, primarily the Traverse City Record-Eagle.

As a freelancer, he's branched out into other media and has reported and produced many stories for Interlochen Public Radio and has had his work broadcast on NPR and Michigan Radio, as well. His work has appeared in the Detroit Free Press, the New York Daily News, traverseticker.com, Traverse Magazine and others.

He's won journalistic awards in investigative reporting, feature writing, breaking news and for writing a humor column.

TO READ MORE, LOOK FOR THESE TITLES

Bath Massacre: America's First School Bombing, by Arnie Bernstein

Blood in the Snow: The True Story of a Stay-at-Home Dad, his High-Powered Wife and the Jealousy That Drove Him to Murder, by Tom Henderson

Blood Justice: The True Story of Multiple Murder and a Family's Revenge, by Tom Henderson

The Burning Bed, by Faith McNulty

Darker than Night, by Tom Henderson

Daylight in the Swamp, by Robert W. Wells

Death's Door: The Truth Behind Michigan's Largest Mass Murder, by Steve Lehto

The Detroit Almanac: 300 years of life in the Motor City, by Peter Gavrilovich and Bill McGraw

The Detroit Mob: And the Disappearance of James Riddle Hoffa, by Robert Grey Reynolds Jr.

The Detroit True Crime Chronicles: Tales of Murder and Mayhem in the Motor City, by Scott M. Burnstein

Devil's Night, by Ze'ev Chafets

Early Organized Crime in Detroit, by James Buccellato

Great Lakes Crime: Murder, Mayhem, Booze & Broads, by Frederick Stonehouse

A Hanging in Detroit: Stephen Gifford Simmons and the Last Execution Under Michigan Law, by David G. Chardavoyne

Haunts of Mackinac: Ghost Stories, Legends & Tragic Tales of Mackinac Island, by Todd Clements

Isadore's Secret: Sin, Murder and Confession in a Northern Michigan Town, by Mardi Link

It Happened in Michigan: Remarkable Events that Changed History, by Colleen Burcar

Living on Sisu: The 1913 Union Copper Strike Tragedy, by Deborah K. Frontiera

Masquerade: A True Story of Seduction, Compulsion and Murder, by Lowell Cauffiel

Michigan Rogues, Desperadoes and Cut-Throats, by Tom Powers

Michigan's Strychnine Saint: The Curious Case of Mrs. Mary McKnight, by Tobin T. Buhk

The Purple Gang.

Motor City Mafia: A Century of Organized Crime in Detroit (Images of America), by Scott M. Burnstein

Murder in Battle Creek: The Mysterious Death of Daisy Zick, by Blaine L. Pardoe and David B. Schock

Murder in Grosse Pointe Park: Privilege, Adultery, and the Killing of Jane Bashara, by Steve Miller

Murder in Michigan's Upper Peninsula, by Sonny Longtine

Murder, Michigan: Seventy fascinating and dramatic murders that have violently shaped the dark side of Michigan history, by Gary W. Barfknecht

Mystery of the Missing Nun: and other famous Michigan murder mysteries, by Larry Wakefield

Once in a Great City: A Detroit Story, by David Maraniss

Poisoning the Pecks of Grand Rapids: The Scandalous 1916 Murder Plot, by Tobin T. Buhk

The Purple Gang: Organized Crime in Detroit 1910-1945, by Paul R. Kavieff

Secret Witness: The Untold Story of the 1967 Bombing in Marshall, Michigan, by Blaine L. Pardoe

Shortcut: The Seeberville Murders and the Dark Side of the American Dream, by Steve Lehto

A Slaying in the Suburbs: the Tara Grant Murder, by Andrea Billups and Steve Miller

The Sweater Letter, by Dave Distel and Lynn Distel

To Hell I Must Go: The True Story of Michigan's Lizzie Borden, by Rod Sadler

True Crime: Michigan - The State's Most Notorious Criminal Cases, by Tobin T. Buhk

When Evil Came to Good Hart, by Mardi Link

Wicked Ottawa County, by Amberrose Hammond

INDEX

MORE FROM MISSION POINT PRESS

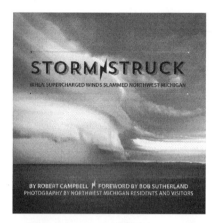
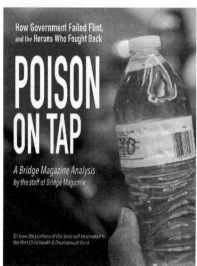
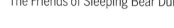

Made in the USA
Middletown, DE
24 July 2022